Pause

Rethinking Leadership to Cultivate Healthy Workplace Cultures

by Karen Mason

Printed in the United Kingdom

First Printing, 2019

ISBN 978-1-9160846-2-9 (Print)
ISBN 978-1-9160846-3-6 (eBook)

Librotas Books
Portsmouth, Hampshire
PO2 9NT

www.Librotas.com

Pause

Pause has a vital message for all leaders: slow down... stop for a moment... rethink how you are leading. If you are ready to challenge yourself, to reflect on your impact as a leader, and to create a healthy environment in which people flourish, then this practical and engaging book is essential reading.

— Madeleine Allen, Managing Director
Allen Training Associates Ltd.

As leaders we can often forget that it is the small things that make the big difference...

Pause resets our thinking around improving organisational performance. It does so by asking us to take time to understand the impact of our interactions with those around us. We are asked to consider ideas to become more effective in our influence. Ultimately impacting on our own, our team's and our organisation's performance.

— Nicholas Lindsey, Information Manager
Royal Hospital for Neuro-disability

In writing this ambitious book Karen has set out to challenge leadership conventions; if leadership matters to you, then *Pause* will resonate. Karen's honesty and visionary approach is insightful, innovative, but above all accessible. Providing the reader with a usable guide to address that most complex of issues, the leadership of people. I took a simple message away: change your habits and you will not only change your future for the better, but the future of the people around you.

— Philip Dyer, Founder
Healthy Leaders

Leadership can be messy and complicated. *Pause* encourages you to recognise "That's okay!" and by giving yourself time to reflect, be honest and vulnerable about what drives you, you can bring about positive personal and organisation change.

— Kieran O'Flaherty, HR Manager
British Film Institute

If you are frustrated by conventional management styles and techniques and want to do something about it, Karen will tell you how. This is a manual for moving you and your colleagues to enjoyable, satisfying, high levels of performance.

— Simon Dixon, CEO
Hatmill

Pause will make you do just that. We all need time to think - whether it's about the future, a current issue or a project you're working on; quality thinking time makes all the difference. Through real stories and anecdotes, theory and questions to make you think, *Pause* will help you recognise patterns from your work environment and get you started on the path to make time for yourself. When you do that, you'll definitely reap the benefits!

— Lorna Murphy, Operations Director
Abellio London Bus

Dedication

For Aaron and Rhys

You are my inspiration.

Foreword

As a director and senior leader of a well-established UK company, I found myself in the middle of what could only be described as a toxic workplace culture. The business was steeped in traditional values. With it came a hierarchical and autocratic leadership approach. The company was led from the top down.

Whilst the senior leaders were purely focused on improving the company's financial position, the people within were suffering and ultimately not engaged, myself included. I knew instinctively there had to be a better way, but I wasn't sure how. My intuition led me to enrol on a development programme, which is how I met Karen. What followed initiated a personal journey of transformation and evolution.

I developed the ability to practise self-reflection, engage with people on a deeper level and inspire them to find purpose and meaning in their work. Reflecting on the messages Karen shares in her book has had a profound influence on how I now choose to lead. A change in values has prompted a shift in my attitude towards my team. As a result we are experiencing significant improvement in productivity and engagement in the work we do together.

Experiencing immense frustration and confusion in my role as a senior leader has led me on a journey of self-discovery. All it took was time to pause and the opportunity to rethink my leadership approach. Along with a little open-mindedness and a sense that there must be a more human way to achieve our business goals.

Through Karen's wisdom and passion for writing, I encourage you to do the same.

Enjoy the journey.

Lewis Smales
Commercial Director

Contents

Prologue

It's 09:00 and the tension in the room is palpable. Smartly dressed men and women are already gathered around the board table. There's nervous laughter as they engage in pleasantries. I arrive, hot and flustered, having dropped my boys at the school gate as early as I dared. The board review is about to start.

There's a knot in my stomach. These reviews are always tough. Knowing I am well prepared isn't enough. My team are outstanding, and I am confident they have prepared as well as humanly possible. However, I can't be sure what challenges I will face during the review.

Slide after monotonous slide, messages begin to merge. The air bristles as it becomes clear that targets are being missed. No one has any control over this project. Tempers fray and there are heated exchanges. I try to remain calm. The pressure builds, with my turn to present still to come.

My heart longs for this creeping death to end.

***

Both my higher education and early working life has been steeped in highly directive, command and control behaviours. I tried desperately to belong, to fit into this environment. Compromising my values, and losing sight of who I really was, took its toll.

Forcing myself to be in this environment literally drained the life from me. For a while my life was being lived from a place of constant fear and anxiety. I dreaded Monday mornings, loathing my short journey to work. My life became a downward spiral leading to depression. Mood swings impacted those I love most, my family.

When I look back it was my doctor who sowed the seeds for change. His advice: if you can't change your environment, change your environment! His message didn't land at first. Intuitively I knew I was to bring change to the culture. I changed role, enthused that at last I would be able to influence a transformation. This was an incredible opportunity to bring a fresh, wholesome approach.

I realise now what I yearned to do was to bring more creativity, support and balance to the dominant, challenging directive leadership style. I naturally bring the best out in people by forming collaborative relationships. Motivated by my new assignment, I was driven to research and discover how to implement a sustainable coaching approach.

Sadly, I failed!

Ill-prepared, I faced an impossible task trying to convince the male board that there was a need for change. At this point I had to face one of the toughest values-based decisions of my life. Knowing this was my work in the world, I chose to leave the organisation.

My personal experience led me to the conclusion that many of our organisations are broken. Traditional ways of working, planning, organising, governance and controls all stifle the human spirit. Our workplace systems are crying out for more human, creative energy and connection to flourish.

I have gone on to work with many leaders across a variety of sectors. Too many have their own stories of how they have disengaged with their own organisation, how they feel disgruntled in their work and unsure what to do about it. Some leave to seek another way; some stay, but find no joy in their work, no longer driven, or able to give the best of themselves.

Such a huge waste of human talent, so is there another way? I truly believe there is. If only you are willing to be brave and make essential changes.

There is a change of tempo in our organisations, a groundswell of change. The world of work is out of balance and many leaders sense this. Our collective intelligence acknowledges the damage we are causing to our planet and ourselves, and we are unsure how to prevent it. It's time to wake up. I believe as leaders we need to pause, to hear the cry for change. It's time to rethink our leadership.

I intend to cause a stir, to bring about wholesale system change to our workplaces, and it starts with you.

This book is a cumulation of my experience since leaving corporate life. During this time I have been researching and facilitating organisation and leadership development. The results prove time after time that reducing hierarchy, whilst adopting a coaching approach to leadership, brings more of what is needed to our organisations: humanity.

Today my work brings me joy as I share my values and beliefs with others. I believe leaders have a responsibility to be self-aware and to evolve in ways that enable work to be productive, fulfilling and meaningful for everybody. I now work with leaders who recognise the need for personal development and positive change in their organisation. I do this by facilitating honest and courageous conversations. I know that in introducing the concepts of a more human approach, to leaders at all levels, makes a real difference.

Thank you for picking up *Pause*. The ideas in the book are intended to prompt you to pause, to think about your own leadership approach, and to support you, your team and organisation to evolve.

I look forward to being alongside you as you explore the possibilities for becoming a more human leader.

How to Use this Book

This practical book has been written for directors, senior leaders and new leaders. My intention through writing this book is to encourage you to develop a reflective practice and to evolve your leadership approach, the results of which will enhance your performance and that of your team.

This book is in three parts.

Part 1: Toxic Cultures

Explores why organisations need to change. Key factors that perpetuate toxic workplace cultures are identified to help you appreciate typical symptoms that need addressing today.

Part 2: Leading on Purpose

Introduces you to three core leadership principles. You are invited to consider how you can develop your style to incorporate these principles in your working practices:

Inspire
… by connecting deeply with your purpose and that of your organisation.

Engage
... you, your team, and wider connections, collaboratively in meaningful work.

Evolve
.... through challenging the way you do things. Identify and implement ways to develop more effective, human practices within your organisation.

Part 3: Cultivating a Healthy Workplace Culture

Practical examples are shared to help you develop a less directive, more human approach to leading. Examples of leadership practices are woven through these chapters. These examples are intended to help you appreciate how adopting a coaching approach, more of the time, enhances your performance as a leader and that of your team.

Pause for thought...

Throughout this book you will be encouraged to pause for thought about your own practice as a leader. There are reflective questions for you to consider. Giving yourself time to reflect will help you to identify your attitude towards the topic being shared. With deeper thought you will start to identify ingrained, habitual patterns of behaviour. The questions posed are intended to raise your awareness and give you choice about changes you want to make.

Through this style of inquiry you can choose the habits you want to hold on to, whilst becoming more conscious of those you want to adapt or let go of. You will be introduced to new practices to replace those that no longer serve you and are out of date.

By pausing to rethink your leadership style, you will evolve as a leader.

Journalling

Journalling is a great way to reflect more deeply and capture your thoughts.

Establishing a routine, where you spend quiet time each day with a notebook and pen can provide you with valuable insights. The act of writing your observations down has the potential to deepen your awareness about your impact on others during the day. Allow your thoughts to flow and simply capture whatever arises.

Over time review your notes to identify any themes, patterns or actions you want to take.

Activity

The best way to evolve as a leader is through practice. I have included activities in this book for you to experiment with your team and colleagues. Give them a go and then take time to reflect and be aware of your impact.

With daily consistency, you will be working in a way that develops and encourages your team members to think for themselves more. This shift in focus enables greater responsibility, autonomy and creativity. When these kinds of conditions are the norm, people thrive in their working environment. Individuals generally want responsibility and to be valued for their skills and talents. As you develop your behaviours, observe how your team start to flourish and performance transforms.

Set your intention daily and make a note in your journal of the belief, skill or behaviour you intend to develop. Keep it simple. Stick with one theme until you feel the change has embedded and you are consistently getting the results you desire.

For example, if you intend to listen to people more, set yourself a goal to catch yourself listening to three people today. Use your reflection time to notice and make brief notes. Here are suggested questions to help you reflect:

- What did you do?
- How did you feel?
- Did you interrupt?
- How comfortable were you with silence?
- What else did you notice about yourself?
- What did you notice about the person or people you were listening to?

Thinking partner or coach

You might find it powerful to find yourself a thinking partner or an experienced coach.

Working with a thinking partner gives you the opportunity to take it in turns to support one another to think through your responses to the questions posed. Your thinking partner is likely to be a peer who would find value in exploring these reflective questions too. Together you can generate new ideas to experiment with and hold one another to account.

The partnering process is a simple one:

1. Agree how long each of you will have to think about a specific question you want to explore, typically 5-10 minutes.
2. The person thinking first shares their thoughts out loud to the question being posed. Your partner pays you their full attention, listening without interruption or asking any questions. This is your time to explore and make sense of your thoughts.

You then swap turns.

This is a great way to practise your listening skills, whilst paying quality attention to one another, a theme you will come across again later in this book.

Alternatively, you can work with an experienced coach to undertake a programme of leadership development using the themes in this book as a framework.

Introduction

If ever there was a time when we needed to reinvent our organisations, it is now. The latest Health and Safety Executive reports[1] claim that work-related stress has reached epidemic proportions. Employee engagement is reported by Gallup[2] to be woefully low. Surely with regular reports such as these, there is a deafening cry for change?

Weekly headlines raise awareness of the problems faced by organisations: disengagement, low productivity rates and talent shortages. With employee wellbeing adversely impacted, a dramatic shift in leadership behaviour is needed. What can be done to cultivate a healthy workplace culture?

Tremendous opportunity exists once senior leaders start to acknowledge they are contributing to this workplace crisis.

Choosing to explore how you lead, and becoming more aware, is a valuable place to start, recognising that outdated leadership approaches contribute to these problems and need to be challenged. With practices being so ingrained it is sometimes difficult to identify the unhelpful attitudes and behaviours that are impacting on performance and wellbeing.

When personal change is perceived as developing "soft skills" and somehow unimportant, or optional, these unhelpful practices remain unchallenged. The responsibility for leaders to be more self-aware has never been greater in terms of potential business benefit. Organisations that fail to take leadership development seriously are fundamentally impacting their bottom line.

Without doubt a different style of leadership is evolving and is vital for the sustainability of many organisations. You have a choice to embrace the changes necessary to become a better leader or continue to contribute to the problem. If you never take time to think about your impact, and be open to new patterns of behaviour, how will you cultivate the conditions for your organisation to flourish?

My intention by writing this book is to build a compelling case for a less directive, more coaching style of leadership, eliminating micromanagement and training people to think for themselves.

Culture change for most organisations is not optional but essential. As a leader, fostering a culture where your employees feel valued and trusted is your key to future success. People in your team want to make a difference. They want to perform and contribute to something they believe in: a worthwhile cause, service or product. It is bureaucracy and behaviours that harm culture and prevent teams from performing at their best.

Reinventing your organisation to cultivate a healthy workplace culture starts by acknowledging you have a need to evolve. Once this is explicit, you can engage in open and honest conversations to explore and focus on introducing new ways of leading.

PART ONE:

Toxic Cultures

"If your actions inspire others to
dream more, learn more, do more
and become more, you are a leader."

John Quincy Adams

CHAPTER ONE:

What's Wrong with Our Organisations?

***

*H*ere we go again. Steve was mocking Naz, a new team member, for a mistake he had found on some paperwork. Steve is our office manager, and he's great at firing off multiple, detailed instructions, without taking a breath to ask if Naz understands what he requires.

Overwhelmed, Naz turned to look over to me, eyebrows raised, looking flushed and helpless. Steve missed the glance in his hurry to get back to his desk. Over time Steve's behaviour has taken its toll on Naz. Naz, feeling unable to speak up, has really started to doubt his ability. It's become a downward spiral; as his confidence has tumbled more mistakes are made.

It wasn't just Naz who felt the brunt of Steve's behaviour. I've also been told, many a time, how to go about completing tasks in minute detail, tasks I'm fully capable of thinking through for myself. They would add stretch and enjoyment to my role. The pleasure from work surely is to be trusted to tap into your own knowledge, experience and creativity?

I enjoy meeting with clients outside the office; here I am free to think on my feet and make decisions. This is what keeps me going. The days I'm office-bound I leave the workplace feeling stifled and my energy is low.

***

Knowing how to get the best from individuals is a challenge many leaders face. People are often promoted into positions of management because they are talented at what they do technically. The challenge comes because they are not necessarily talented at getting the best from others, or even have the desire to. These new managers are often set up to fail.

Left to their own devices, these managers receive minimal development and must learn on the job. They are expected to know how to tap into the potential of their team and be good leaders. Knowing no better, these leaders often end up modelling the traditional "command and control", habitual behaviours of more senior leaders around them. Keen to pass on their expertise, they perpetuate an outdated style of leadership that no longer serves us well.

Without pausing to challenge these behaviours, what often occurs is the opposite of what is needed. Without recognising the need for personal development these leaders, rather than igniting the potential within their team members, unwittingly perpetuate a toxic workplace environment.

I hear many stories like the one above. It is typical of the kind of behaviour experienced in many organisations. It is not surprising therefore that low morale and lack of engagement are often cited as significant problems facing organisations. These issues ultimately contribute to low productivity and performance.

The prevalence of a command and control style of leadership is steeped in our history, proving to be such a successful approach when adopted by military leaders over many hundreds of years. This style of leadership helped to win battles and wars. As military leaders moved into businesses in the mid-1900s, they brought this proven style with them and it is now woven into the fabric of many traditional organisations. The trouble today, in our fast changing workplaces, is that this style of leadership constrains autonomy, thinking and creativity. It prevents individuals from bringing their whole selves to work and fulfilling their potential. Hierarchies infantilise, contributing to a parent-child style of relationships. This style of leadership rarely brings out the best in people. People want to be treated as adults, trusted to think for themselves, and have autonomy to act in the moment.

Here, another example of poor leadership and micromanagement is shared, leading to employee disengagement...

***

My manager feels the need to direct and control everything I do. She even stands over my shoulder and instructs me what to write in my email responses. She doesn't trust me, and so I've switched off. There's no point wasting my energy thinking about how to respond to challenges and situations. My manager won't let me do it my way, and I will never be good enough. It has to be done the way she wants it doing.

***

Anger and resentment are clear. The interference and micromanagement by the manager are not welcome. Sadly, the person sharing her story doesn't have the courage to have a conversation with her manager to explore how it could be usefully different. Without an honest conversation, this relationship is not going to improve.

Our organisations are growing in complexity, with rapid access to data and information. They are dynamic in ways unimaginable in the past, and yet we hold on to this outdated way of leading. It is no longer realistic that one person can be the hub, holding all the answers, knowing what needs to be done to optimise performance. Responsibility needs to be devolved and shared with the people closest to the source of information. Outdated leadership behaviours, whilst deeply ingrained in many of our organisations, need to be challenged for organisations to evolve.

Recognising some of the limiting traits of command and control leadership is a useful place to start to raise your awareness as a leader. Knowing the beliefs that underpin your behaviours enables you to challenge your mindset and introduce change. So, what are some of the traits these traditional leaders demonstrate?

- They know best... demonstrated by a lack of listening, and interrupting to get their point across.

- They set direction... holding on tightly to predetermined plans which they expect will deliver results. This is often poorly communicated with limited engagement. There may be rigidity, and no room for creativity or flexibility as information emerges that requires deviation from the plan.

- They require control mechanisms... in the form of copious and time-consuming reports. This data is used to review the past and minimise deviance from the plan. With so much focus on the past, it leaves little, if any, time to notice if they are still heading in the direction they want to travel. Opportunities are missed to work in the here and now, and identify what adjustments are needed for the future.

- They are inflexible to change. A need for change implies leadership failure and that the leader did not plan thoroughly enough!

In today's world these kind of behaviours stifle productivity, engagement and creativity. Instead they breed distrust and form the foundations of unhealthy, toxic cultures.

A recent example of how a toxic culture has negatively impacted the reputation of a well-known organisation is that of Amnesty International. Here an independent investigation into the suicides of two employees revealed signs that all was not well within the organisation. The staff wellbeing review[3] highlights how even an organisation with high ideals can succumb to unhealthy practices, with over a third of its staff reporting that working for the charity has caused them health problems.

Leading an organisation which espouses good intentions and values is only helpful if those leading the organisation hold themselves to account. It is essential to incorporate practices that ensure these values are lived throughout.

So often leaders are too busy to know what is really happening within their organisation. It is only by taking time to pause and listen to people, that you get a real sense of what is happening at an operational level.

If you deny yourself the time to truly connect with people you will miss key signals - signals telling you behaviours in your system are not as they should be. Worse still, if left unaddressed these behaviours have the potential to damage the wellbeing of your people and the reputation of your organisation.

Pause for thought...

In your own experience, what examples have you seen of toxic leadership actions, attitudes or behaviours?

What examples have you seen of effective leadership actions, attitudes or behaviours?

How do these traits impact performance?

CHAPTER TWO:

Organisational Dis-ease

"If you always do what you've
always done, you'll always get
what you've always got."

Henry Ford

Having explored some of the ideas that have determined why our organisations have become unhealthy places to work, in this chapter I will explore in more detail some of the factors that contribute to creating toxic workplace cultures.

This is a valuable opportunity to take time to recognise how these problems can become a downward spiral, and self-fulfilling. It is an opportunity for leaders to wake up and take responsibility for the impact of their behaviour.

During my experience of being a leader within an organisation, and working as an external change facilitator, I have come across four significant factors that negatively impact the health of an organisation:

1. Results are all that matter.
2. There is a lack of shared purpose.
3. People don't feel valued or recognised.
4. Leaders lack self-awareness.

Let's look at each of these in turn...

Results, results, results

"I have a foundational belief that business results start with culture and your people."

Douglas Conant

Results are the primary focus and priority for many organisations, so much so that the leaders in these organisations consistently prioritise performance delivery over people. These organisations are structured to control performance and results, which leads to an environment rather like a "corporate straightjacket". Here people are unable to think for themselves, having to blindly follow processes to ensure results are achieved predictably. People work in silos, focused and rewarded for their individual contribution.

The consequence of this approach is a lack of appreciation for the wider system in which they operate. This shows up as limited awareness of how individual actions impact others. I have had many conversations with leaders who are so focused on achieving personal targets, to achieve their individual bonus, that they give no thought to the impact of their actions on their wider team, organisation or society.

Hierarchy is intended to provide control through top-down, parental-style decision making. This structure becomes a bottleneck as organisations grow and become victims of their own success. The hierarchy becomes a mechanism in which decisions and accountability may be avoided. Senior leaders make the key decisions, whilst team members wait for instruction and authorisation. These are the same employees who are often best placed to make decisions in relation to the source of information that needs to be acted upon. Yet they are unable to productively engage in what they know to be right for their organisation as they do not have the authority.

Leaders who command required performance in an attempt to control results are often unaware that instead they are choking productivity and stifling creativity. This style of leadership creates an environment where people are not trusted to do their best work. Individuals are unable to make decisions, and feel challenged and unsupported.

As organisations grow, they become more bureaucratic with the introduction of control mechanisms. Associated behaviours proliferate to prevent mistakes being made, such as review meetings to check up on performance. Consequently people stop taking responsibility, deferring to policy and procedure and often blaming others for mistakes. People in this kind of environment stop thinking for themselves. This ultimately results in a significant lack of productivity.

According to the Gallup 2017 State of the Global Workplace report only 11% of UK employees are engaged in their job, compared with 70% in the world's most successful organisations. Something needs to change.

Pause for thought...

Where is your focus?

Take a moment to consider, are your conversations with team members mainly about:

Performance and targets?

How things get done and the processes being employed?

Asking what ideas your team have to progress an activity?

What leadership behaviours do you notice are most prevalent in your organisation?

How productive do you perceive your organisation to be? What are the signs?

Lack of shared purpose

*"If you don't know where you are
going, any road will get you there."*

Lewis Carroll

As leaders, in order to bring people with you, you need to be clear about why your organisation exists and the direction you intend to travel.

For people to be inspired and motivated by their work they need to align with the purpose of your organisation. However, very often when asked about the purpose of their organisation it's not at all clear. Without a clear sense of purpose that individuals feel aligned with, it is hard for them to find meaning and direction in their work.

People often share how busy they are at work, but they don't feel like they are achieving anything worthwhile. This can lead to a real sense of frustration, which impacts motivation.

How often have you got to the end of the week and felt frustrated by what appears to be a lack of any real progress? Maybe you have spent a considerable proportion of your week in meetings and responding to email. You haven't had a chance to carve out time to work on that key project deliverable you intended to start when you arrived at work on Monday, or hold that important conversation with your colleague. This lack of focus on clear outcomes is as a result of getting caught up with distractions and other people's priorities. It drains energy, hugely impacting your ability to perform and feel satisfied by your work. It may well leave you feeling frazzled.

How clear are you about what needs doing in your role and how to go about it?

Many people have vague goals that have been imposed. When this happens there is little sense of ownership or commitment. This, along with a lack of role clarity, has a significant impact on productivity and job satisfaction.

Pause for thought...

Does your organisation share a clear message about why it exists?

How much ownership do you have of your current goals?

When you think about how you are going to achieve your goals, who do you need to involve for the knowledge and experience they bring?

How do you engage with these people?

Lack of communication

"The single biggest problem in communication is the illusion that it has taken place."

George Bernard Shaw

One of the most commonly reported issues I hear when running leadership development programmes is how ineffective communication is in a particular organisation. Communication is a big topic and when I enquire about the specific problems being experienced examples often include:

- Communication is one way i.e. top down.
- Outcomes are imposed and rarely discussed.
- We don't know what's going on.
- I'm not sure what is expected of me.
- No one listens to me.
- I don't feel appreciated.
- My manager is not utilising my strengths.
- I'm not being developed in my role.

Leaders are often so focused on the delivery of targets and attempting to control performance that they forget about the needs of the people they work with. They forget to invest time in building a relationship and really getting to know people as individuals. This can lead to an environment of high challenge, where people feel exposed and unsupported.

Communication generally improves when you shift your focus and show interest in people first. Start to build relationships which say to the person you are with, "you matter". When people sense this genuine interest and recognition, they feel recognised and valued. When you demonstrate their contribution matters, people often go the extra mile to perform.

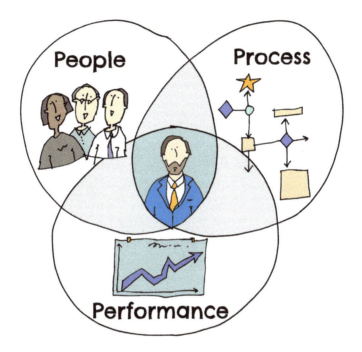

Pause for thought...

When you initiate a conversation with a colleague, how do you usually start the conversation?

What can you say to show a genuine interest in the person?

How often do you discuss individual aspirations and development?

What opportunities do you have to grow and develop your team?

Lack of self-awareness

"People leave managers, not companies."

Marcus Buckingham

Sadly, one of the biggest problems in our organisations are leaders who lack self-awareness. These leaders may think they have the qualities required to be a good leader and yet are often unaware of the impact they have on those around them. For those who do have awareness, they may be unsure how to adapt their style to bring the best out of the people around them. These leaders rarely prioritise their own development or pause to reflect on their impact.

One of the topics that frequently arises in coaching is a need to explore how to improve a poor relationship with a manager. Coachees often seek to develop their thinking about how they can improve the relationship or leave their job. The impact of poor relationships does untold damage within organisations, often a source of workplace stress, sickness and absenteeism, or presenteeism (where an individual is turning up for work but not engaged).

There is a real need for leaders to recognise that organisations don't change, it is the people within them who do. As a leader it is important to lead by example. Demonstrating a willingness to develop yourself is a great place to start. You can then support others to be the change you want reflected in a functional, high performing organisation. Your role as a leader is to bring the best out in others and harness the huge amount of talent and potential in your organisation.

Pause for thought...

When was the last time you undertook some form of personal development and what did you learn?

How open and honest are your relationships with peers and colleagues?

When was the last time you actively sought personal feedback?

You're not listening

When we perceive key people around us are not listening and our views and opinions are not being heard, our wellbeing can be hugely impacted. If this situation goes on for any length of time, the damage to our self-esteem and performance is untold. This was borne out by an experience recently shared with me.

***

The atmosphere at work is grim. Deadlines are being missed, targets failed and my thoughts about how to turn the project around are being ignored. My line manager thinks he knows best. He fires off his orders via email and expects the team to run with his instructions, without question.

No one believes in what they are being asked to do. I've tried to give him feedback, but he just doesn't listen. It feels futile.

His controlling behaviour has become overbearing. I am desperately trying to salvage the project, but the team are sinking, and sinking fast. The lack of self-awareness being shown by my manager and his impact on the team is proving too much. I'm not the only one at breaking point.

I'm not sure what can be done to turn this situation around.

The only person I can change is myself and my approach. Whilst I can try to influence my manager, I cannot make him change. I feel stuck...

***

If Arul is unable to change his relationship with his manager, he may take the decision to leave. Sadly, many do.

As a leader, it's important to recognise that people need to be heard; it's a basic human need. Your team need to know they matter and are valued. This doesn't mean you have to agree with everything that is said. It does mean you need to make time for others: time to understand your similarities and differences and to find ways to move forward together. When conflict exists, it needs to be examined, not ignored in the hope it will magically go away. It rarely does.

We will explore levels of listening in Part 3 and if there is one thing you take away from reading this book, I encourage you to develop the quality of your listening. It will make the biggest impact on your experience at work and that of your team. As human beings we all yearn to be heard.

You are not alone

Ben arrived a little bemused on the first day of the programme. He checked in and shared his story.

***

I'm not really sure why I'm here. I work hard in my family business. We're all running around like headless chickens. I often stop and wonder what it's all for!

The senior leaders are unaware of the issues in the organisation. They bury their heads in the sand, focused on performance and results. They don't really care how we treat our people, so long as we deliver a profit. The fallout is everyone comes to me with their gripes and moans about how they are being treated as employees. People are starting to vote with their feet, taking time off sick or leaving. I do think there is a better way to lead in the business and a better way to tell people what to do.

***

What was ironic about Ben's check-in was that he really had no idea that he was embarking on a leadership development programme that would enable him to flex his style and transform his relationship with his team. He was about to develop skills that would enable his team to think for themselves and take greater responsibility for their actions, a far cry from learning how to "tell them what to do"!

The key to Ben's success was that he arrived with an open mind and a willingness to try new approaches. The rest is history.

Does working in your organisation bring you joy? If not, would you like to bring about positive change? You are not alone.

There is a growing movement of people who know that the way we organise is ineffective and unsustainable. However, they are unclear what the alternative is. Increasingly in my work I notice leaders who are challenging old methods of leadership. Intuitively they know what worked in the past is no longer working. They need to learn to flex their style. With limited role models to show them how, these leaders can become disillusioned, unsure how to change. Like Ben, those who are sufficiently disgruntled are proactively seeking out new ways, reading the many articles and books available via social media and embarking on programmes of personal development with a coach or as part of a wider leadership development programme. Recognising the value of development is an important step. Acknowledging you don't always get things right at work and are open to discovering new ways of leading can be a breakthrough moment.

CHAPTER THREE:

So What's the Alternative?

We live in volatile and uncertain times. There is a real opportunity to be part of a growing movement intending to bring greater humanity to our failing organisations. It's time to expand your thinking and enable yourself and your colleagues to flourish, cultivating healthy organisations that care about you and your wellbeing and tap into your potential.

It's time to challenge limiting beliefs about how to lead and support one another to perform well. Successful leaders are self-aware and willing to flex their style. They are ready to develop and adopt positive changes in their behaviour. Through developing a growth mindset, you can evolve yourselves and your organisations. What is needed are leaders who are willing to create a safe space for brave and courageous conversations, who challenge the status quo, are comfortable with not knowing the answer and are ready to experiment with new ways of being, to bring out the best in everybody.

Take time to reflect on the four key issues I shared in the previous chapter that underpin the need for change:

1. Results are all that matter.
2. There is a lack of shared purpose.

3. Poor communication means that people don't feel valued or recognised.

4. Leaders lack self-awareness.

If you recognise one or more of these issues in your organisation, you can make a difference by changing what is happening. You can challenge the status quo by choosing to be courageous, by showing up and being different. This may well require you to be open to a shift in your own thinking and behaviour. Read on to discover how many successful leaders are evolving.

In Part 2 of this book I share knowledge and experience from the many leadership development programmes I have facilitated. My intention is to give you a starting point for your own development. Here is my three-step approach to help you develop your thinking as a leader:

1. **Inspire:** by creating a compelling sense of purpose. Discover how to give work meaning and direction for others.

2. **Engage:** by adopting behaviours which, when you connect with people, say "you matter". Learn to engage in a way that fosters trust, recognises strengths and encourages greater autonomy. Discover how to bring out the leader in people throughout your organisation.

3. **Evolve:** by recognising the world is not standing still. Become more self-aware, constructively challenge outdated practices and continually seek to develop yourself, along with those around you.

In this next section I invite you to consider and develop practices that enable you to connect more meaningfully with your colleagues. I encourage you to be more human in your workplace. With a focus on developing connection with your team first, you will build an environment of trust. Through this trust, know that you will be working on the things that matter, and performance and results will follow.

Call to action

Traditional performance management and action planning are doing little to resolve the chronic problems faced by many organisations. So, what if you change your focus? Instead of focusing on problems, such as missed targets, what if you develop an approach to truly connect with the solution? This is the solution experienced when you harness the talents of the people in your organisation.

If the culture in your organisation feels dysfunctional, or worse, toxic, trust yourself, be open to learning and find the courage needed to model a different way. When you become clear about your purpose, you become more intentional. With a renewed sense of direction you can be the change needed to influence the next stage of development within your organisation. So much can be achieved when you learn to adapt your style and approach, when you discover how to inspire, engage and evolve as a leader within your organisation.

Read on to discover how to connect more deeply with the people you work with, in a way that liberates their full potential.

PART TWO:

Leading on Purpose

"There's no magic formula for
great company culture. The key
is just to treat your staff how
you would like to be treated."

Richard Branson

There is no blueprint, or as Richard Branson says, no magic formula, to creating a healthy workplace culture, a place where people and performance flourish.

What is required are leaders who are leading on purpose – leaders who are driven by the purpose of their organisation, equipped with self-awareness, along with a willingness to flex and change. These are the leaders who will get the best from everyone around them. These leaders need a desire to trust and engage with others, whilst letting go of more traditional beliefs, and discouraging or replacing procedures that prevent people being their best at work.

This work starts within. Examine what energises you as a leader, your purpose.

It's Monday morning and you are heading to work... imagine you arrive:

- Energised by the values of your organisation and wholly committed to its purpose,
- Knowing you are valued for your contribution,
- Excited about engaging in productive and meaningful conversations,
- Believing you make a difference,
- Expecting to enjoy your day!

... and so, this is my aspiration for you, and for people at work everywhere!

I am inspired to provide a service that helps leaders cultivate a healthy workplace culture, where people matter. I do this by supporting leaders, like you, to become more self-aware and take ownership to drive positive change throughout your workplace. This gives me my energy along with a sense of purpose and direction. It informs the actions I choose to take, each and every day. In Part 2 I'll be sharing ideas and coaching questions to encourage you to pause and discover how you can bring about the positive changes you imagine for yourself and your organisation. This isn't about changing others; it's all about you and what you can do to bring about change. Reading this part of the book you can expect:

- Your thinking to be challenged,
- To explore empowering beliefs,
- To practise new ways of being with your colleagues and team.

I will now develop the three themes I have previously mentioned to support your thinking and develop you as a leader:

- How you **inspire** others
- How you **engage** others
- How you **evolve** as a leader

Inspire

This is your starting point and an opportunity to consider how you inspire your team and wider stakeholders. Here I introduce you to three practices to inspire others.

- Find purpose
- Establish values
- Envisage your outcomes

To inspire others you need to find your **purpose** and know why your organisation exists. In Chapter 4 you will find coaching questions to enable you to tap into your purpose and discover how you align with the purpose of your organisation. There are personal activities for you to complete and activities to engage your team and wider organisation.

Next, you will consider what is most important to you about your work and that of your organisation. This chapter invites you to think about your core **values** and those of your organisation. Again, you have the chance to reflect on how well these are in alignment with one another.

Finally, I will introduce you to the concept of **outcomes**. Here you will discover how focusing on what you want is a powerful way to co-create a vision with your team and engage them in its delivery.

Engage

Organisations that fail to engage their employees suffer from significant shortfalls in productivity and performance. In Chapter 5 I will offer practices to enable you to engage well with your team and wider connections. These are:

- Importance of connection
- Foster autonomy
- Conditions to flourish

How you relate to others and **connect**, either one to one or in groups, has a huge bearing on how successful you will be at engaging people. In this chapter there will be coaching questions and examples to enable you to consider your attitudes and behaviours, providing an opportunity for you to think about the impact you make on others.

Encouraging greater **autonomy** through freedom to think, and building trust, is fundamental to engaging others. This happens when you pause to recognise the leadership potential in everyone around you whilst seeking to develop a high performing team. Challenging bureaucracy and rules about what people can and can't do is central to empowering others. Developing people to enable them to think for themselves, and take responsibility for their actions, is a huge opportunity for greater engagement and performance.

Creating conditions in which people **flourish** is about enabling people to come to work to be creative. The future success of your organisation is based on your ability to adapt and change, your ability to meet the ever-evolving needs of your clients and environment. Your survival depends on people keeping an open mind as to what the future holds, feeling free to experiment to find out what works and discard what doesn't. People need to feel safe to explore their ideas, without fear of reprisal or blame. These are the conditions required for people to flourish in the workplace. Workplaces benefit immensely from encouraging creativity.

Evolve

Ensuring you evolve your practice as a leader keeps you fresh and enables your organisation to evolve with you. If you fail to give yourself time to recharge, refresh and renew your thinking, you become trapped in an outdated world.

In Chapter 6 I will suggest concepts and coaching questions for you to explore your own development along with that of your team. You will be encouraged to consider:

- Be you
- Positive beliefs
- Choose your focus

Being you is about recognising what you are good at and doing more of it. Know your strengths, and those of your team, and you can then support one another to optimise talents. Working with your strengths and creating stretch to develop talent encourages personal growth. It increases your performance and positively impacts those around you. When you focus on tapping into strengths, and adjust roles accordingly, it optimises how people perform.

A key requirement of good leadership is self-awareness. The more aware you are of your attitudes and **beliefs**, which inform your habits and behaviours, the greater choice you have over how you impact others. This chapter provides coaching questions for you to reflect on your beliefs. You will learn to recognise internal interference that prevents you from being the best leader you can be.

The phrase "energy flows where attention goes" is a useful reminder to be careful where you **choose** to place **your focus** and choose your attitude. Your focus has a significant impact on what gets done and how. When you focus on problems you can get stuck in the problem and struggle to make decisions and move forward, losing time and energy. When you shift your focus to explore solutions, the energy shifts too. In this chapter I will share an approach to help you maintain a positive focus that delivers results.

CHAPTER FOUR:

Inspire

"Efforts and courage are not enough
without purpose and direction."

John F. Kennedy

To inspire others, you need to be inspired.

Pause for thought

Consider for a moment, do you feel energised and motivated when you think about your work?

If so

Where does your energy and motivation come from?

What excites you?

If not, spend a few minutes reminding yourself

What brings you joy in your work?

What brings out the best in you?

Once essential needs are met in terms of safety and security, most people start seeking more meaning from their work. This is often unconscious as inadvertently you seek to make a difference to a cause, or further a belief, that's important to you. When this is absent from your work you can often find yourself wondering what it's all for. Doubt sets in as you wonder if you make any significant difference through the work that you do.

The work of Abraham Maslow and his hierarchy of needs is a valuable framework to consider. Once the basic physiological and security needs of your team are satisfied through access to water, air, food, sleep, health, safety and employment, people start to seek something more.

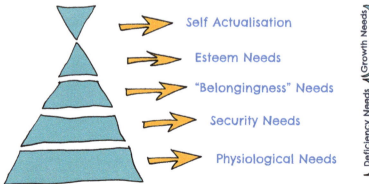

For people to engage and perform to the best of their ability, they need to feel a sense of belonging in order to flourish and grow in their working environment. This is why the way you engage with your team, to create a psychologically safe environment, is vital for the high performance of your team. The theme of engagement will be explored in more detail in Chapter 5, to help you consider how to bring about an essential sense of belonging in your team.

Many of your team will be seeking fulfilment by having their esteem needs met. They need to feel respected, accepted and valued by others. If you are to inspire others, you need to meet their growth needs.

Self-actualisation is achieved when people find their work meaningful. When you experience making a positive contribution, and feel inspired by and aligned with the reason your organisation and team exists, you are working on purpose.

When you feel aligned with the purpose of your organisation you feel motivated by your work. Once purpose is clear people need to appreciate how they are expected to deliver on that purpose. Determining what is important about how you behave with one another, and wider stakeholders, is defined through your values.

Finally, your team need to be clear about what they are setting out to achieve. This requires clearly defined outcomes to give a vision of success and guide actions.

Find purpose

Why does your organisation exist?

To inspire others, you must first connect with your own sense of purpose. With this self-awareness you are then able to recognise how you align and contribute to the purpose of your organisation. For some people this is the start of a realisation that there is no alignment. With growing awareness, they recognise that a change of direction is required for them to find fulfilment.

Establish values

How do you want people to feel about you, your products or services?

Once you are clear about your purpose, why you do what you do, it's time to turn your attention to what's important to you about how you do your work. Knowing what's important helps you to behave congruently with your core personal and organisation values.

Envisage your outcomes

What do you want to deliver?

Having identified your values, it's then good to know in what direction you want to head. Getting clear about your outcomes helps set direction for everyone around you. This helps people know how best to contribute their skills, knowledge and talents to create high performance.

In summary, people perform at their best when they are inspired and sense alignment from within themselves. This is because they are connecting congruently with their role and recognising how they contribute to their team and organisation to meet a need in the world. This is the foundation for cultivating a healthy workplace culture.

Through the work you do reading this chapter you will be able to clarify your own alignment, whilst working with your team to help them align too.

So how will you inspire others?

Let's take each key theme and explore what you can do in more detail.

Find purpose

"Just as people cannot live without eating,
so a business cannot live without profits.

But most people don't live to
eat, and neither must businesses
live just to make profits."

John Mackey

Being explicit about the purpose of your organisation is a valuable opportunity to think about why your organisation exists. Very often the initial response to the question "What is your purpose as an organisation?" is about being profitable or achieving targets. However, making profit for shareholders, or achieving arbitrary targets, is not what inspires most people to come to work. People want something more: they want to be of service, contributing to a worthy cause or belief.

The purpose of an organisation needs to connect with the hearts of its employees, and customers. It needs to be lived. When people feel truly connected to a purpose that is greater than themselves, they feel inspired to come to work. This contributes to a strong sense of belonging, whilst generating greater personal commitment and motivation.

This reminds me of the wonderful story of when John F. Kennedy was visiting NASA. He is reported to have spent hours talking to all the engineers and scientists about their work. As he gets ready to leave, he notices a janitor cleaning the corridor. Kennedy stops to speak to the man, and asks him, "And what is it that you do here?" The janitor replies, "The same as everybody else, sir. I'm helping to put a man on the moon." Whilst the story has been told many times, it is still such a great example of how being on purpose connects and motivates people.

Having worked with groups of leaders to explore the question "What is your purpose as an organisation?" this seemingly simple question runs deep. For some the question proves quite a challenge. Pinpointing a clear response can be elusive. Some will identify what they value, what makes their organisation different, but not be quite able to articulate their deeper purpose.

The value for getting clear about the purpose of your organisation can be huge. Here are three good reasons for leading on purpose:

1. **Contribution**
   When you dig deep, and connect with your true purpose, you unearth the real value your organisation contributes to society.

2. **Alignment**
   Being clear about your purpose is like a beacon. It attracts the people who share your beliefs. This may be your customers, employees, partners or other key stakeholders. When people align with a shared sense of purpose, greater meaning and fulfilment is created in your workplace.

   As an organisation your purpose becomes an integral part of your Unique Selling Proposition (USP), it provides an opportunity to attract talent to your business and sends a clear message to your customers about what they can expect from working with you.

3. **Energy**
   When people contribute to a belief or cause they care about, decisions and actions are more likely to flow. A shared sense of purpose provides a compass reference, guiding the daily choices being made by each and every one of the team. People find themselves energised and motivated when their purpose is clear. In turn, deeper, more meaningful relationships are built between colleagues.

For those organisations who are clear about why they exist, a motivational purpose statement can help to summarise and communicate with employees and wider stakeholders. This statement guides action and helps people make congruent decisions. Being clear about your purpose can be a double-edged sword. Boards sometimes find choices leading to ethical dilemmas, particularly when purpose is at odds with making a profit. Sadly, time and again short-term gain wins over doing the right thing for the long term.

Here are some examples of succinct Purpose Statements.

For McLaren Group it is simply:

"To win."

It's this sense of purpose that has driven the company to its current prominent high-tech, global brand position.

Southwest Airlines state their purpose:

"To connect People to what's important
in their lives through friendly,
reliable, and low-cost air travel."

Both companies have their Purpose Statements clearly visible on their websites. They actively use these statements to lead within their business and guide decision making.

What can you do?

Your purpose is outward looking. It's all about what your organisation does for others. What is the need in the world that is being met by your organisation? So, if you were to think about the context of your organisation, what is its purpose?

Capture your Purpose Statement here...

_____

_____

_____

If it's not clear, this is a significant opportunity to take time out as a leadership team, to be creative and share thinking with your colleagues, whilst allowing a deeper sense of purpose to emerge. Here are some coaching questions to help you think about your purpose.

Who do you serve?

How are you improving the lives of the people you serve?

What is the cause or belief that your organisation is fulfilling?

What problem are you solving?

What do you want to change?

How do you make a difference?

What are you passionate about?

What is the purpose of your organisation?

Which of these questions resonate?

Stick with the questions that enable you to mine deeply for the real reason for your organisation's existence. Capture your succinct statement that defines the essence of your purpose.

Working with my own organisation as an example, here are my responses to these questions...

Who do you serve?

I serve people working in organisations.

How are you improving the lives of the people you serve?

Through my work developing leaders, people have a better experience at work. Their quality of life is improved.

What is the cause or belief that your organisation is fulfilling?

I care deeply about the experiences people have at work. I believe everyone should go home at the end of each day feeling productive and fulfilled.

What do you want to change?

I want to eliminate toxic workplace cultures and instead cultivate healthy cultures, where people matter.

How do you make a difference?

I work with leaders to help raise awareness of the need for change. I do this by introducing ideas and challenging thinking. I create a safe space in which to explore concepts, practise behaving differently and experience transformational results.

What are you passionate about?

I am passionate about equipping leaders with the values, knowledge and skills to let go of controlling behaviours, instead encouraging greater autonomy and cultivating an environment where people take greater responsibility by thinking for themselves.

What problem are you solving?

Toxic workplace cultures are literally draining the life from employees. Workplace absence due to mental health issues, presenteeism, low engagement and poor productivity are the consequence of how we treat one another in the workplace. My work transforms leaders and their approach, inspiring greater engagement and productivity so individuals and organisations flourish and grow.

What is the purpose of your organisation?

To help leaders cultivate healthy workplace cultures where people and performance flourish.

These reflective questions can be valuable to reflect on at any level, be it for yourself, your team or your wider organisation. Once your purpose is defined it's no good simply adding these words to a page, a strapline for posters or on your website. It's important that purpose becomes integral, woven through everything you, your team and organisation do. Purpose needs to underpin every decision you make, who you recruit, the projects you take on, the clients you say "yes" to and the way you organise yourselves.

Once you have defined your purpose you can choose to live it and lead on purpose, bringing it to life in all that you do. As a leader you have the opportunity to lead by example and promote practices such as:

1. Sharing stories regularly with team members to highlight examples of purpose being lived.

2. Encouraging your team to take part in reflective discussions, to share how they connect personally with the wider purpose of your organisation.

3. Finding examples to write about on your social platforms. This may be a great way of connecting with a new client. For example, how did purpose play a part in the way a service is being delivered? Perhaps purpose played a key part in a recent recruitment success? I'm sure you can find many other examples once you start looking!

As your organisation grows and evolves, recognise that your purpose may need to evolve too. Your purpose should be organic, reflecting the nature of environmental change. Accepting what the world needs of you and your organisation today may not be the same in the future.

Pause for thought...

So now it's your turn to vision success. Here is your opportunity to stop and consider your ideal organisation and consider how you will work towards achieving it.

Take time now to imagine... what is your dream for your organisation?

What do you see when your organisation is at its best?

What do you hear?

How do you feel?

This is an opportunity to capture your thoughts for a statement of possibility. Review your answers to the previous three questions and list any keywords that signify what you would like to make possible.

Take a little time to reflect on the choices you have made as a leader. Knowing what you want to achieve is a valuable starting point. It is only by knowing what you want that you can start to disrupt current practices, challenge thinking and change behaviours to bring about your vision.

What might it take to create the kind of organisation that enables people to find more meaning in their work and flourish?

Activity

Aligning with personal purpose

Now is your opportunity to think about your own alignment.

What is important to you?

What do you really care about?

When you can identify with a cause or belief you feel passionate about, this serves to motivate and drive you in all that you do.

How does your purpose align with that of your organisation?

How do you contribute and make a difference at work?

It's important for you to know what you stand for and check how your contribution aligns with your organisation's purpose. When this is clear you will feel more driven and motivated by your work.

Activity

Team alignment activity

This alignment exercise is a great activity to carry out with your team members too. It's a valuable way to engage people in thinking about what motivates them, and how they contribute to your team and wider organisation.

Start the discussion by agreeing how you want to work together. For example, you might agree to respect everyone's input without judgement, listen to people in turn, be self-aware and manage how long you take to share your thoughts. What else would be useful for you to work well together?

The "aligning with personal purpose" questions above are a useful starting point. Invite each of your team to share their responses. Then allow time for discussion. Together, shape what this all means for you as a team: your performance, how you can get the best from one another and how you can contribute to the wider organisation.

Establish values

*"It's not hard to make decisions when
you know what your values are."*

Roy E. Disney

...but tricky to make decisions that align, if you have no values!

Once clear about how you align with the purpose of your organisation, you can establish how you fulfil your purpose. Your values, what you care about, need to be at the heart of everything you do and how you do it. We are often unaware of our lived values as they are deeply ingrained. Knowing your values becomes an opportunity to honour what is important to you and to your organisation. Having clarity informs the way you are with one another in the workplace and beyond.

Conversely, if what is important in the workplace is ambiguous then work can be confusing. Often organisations have espoused values but don't live by them. This leads to uncertainty about what really matters and how you are expected to behave. Operating in such an environment affects our resilience and confidence to perform. If left unchallenged, this kind of environment can become toxic as people face indecision resulting in overwhelm.

People feel compelled to come to work, knowing that they are not giving their best, but are unsure how to change the way it feels at work. Alternatively, people realise this isn't a good environment to work in and they leave. Either way, an incredible amount of talent is wasted due to a lack of clarity leading to confusion.

The opportunity is to develop an organisation in which people clearly know what is important to operate successfully, then live the values that bring alignment. When what is expected is clear you can choose to buy in to what is expected of you, and act confidently and authentically. This congruence leads to personal and organisational wellbeing. When you act on purpose, and in alignment with your values, you can truly be yourself. Whilst work can be demanding and stressful at times, you are more likely to be resilient if you know what's expected and feel confident in your role.

Here are a couple of examples of values statements that underpin the actions and choices of two big brand names.

At **Etsy** their guiding principles are:

We commit to our craft.
We minimise waste.
We embrace differences.
We dig deeper.
We lead with optimism.

Zappos

Deliver WOW Through Service.
Embrace and Drive Change.
Create Fun and A Little Weirdness.
Be Adventurous, Creative, and Open-Minded.
Pursue Growth and Learning.
Build Open and Honest Relationships With Communication.
Build a Positive Team and Family Spirit.
Do More With Less.
Be Passionate and Determined.
Be Humble.

I've chosen these examples as in my experience these simple statements provide employees and customers with clarity about what to expect from these organisations.

A list of words that represent values needs to be explored more deeply for individuals to make sense of what they mean. For example, Procter and Gamble have chosen five words:

1. Integrity
2. Leadership
3. Ownership
4. Passion for Winning
5. Trust

To bring these words to life, more detail about what each of these words mean needs to be explored. This detail can be found on their website. Yet at first glance it isn't clear how these words are embedded in their culture.

Values-led organisations recognise the importance of sharing a set of values. The values provide a moral compass and principles for people to operate by. When values are lived and explicit, everyone knows what is expected of them. Standards are clear and become ingrained, sending out a clear message to your wider community about how you do things. Values help determine your reputation. When people experience values being lived, rather than simply stated, they understand what is expected of them and can align their behaviour accordingly. If what is expected of them is not a good fit, they can consciously make an alternative choice.

People often choose to leave an organisation when dominant behaviours are out of alignment with the stated values of the organisation. If there is an incongruence around stated and lived values, this often results in an unhealthy workplace culture.

Bringing values to life, and living them, is core to you successfully inspiring your team. If you are uncertain what the values of your organisation are, the next section provides you with an activity to work on with your team to help determine them.

Activity

Organisational values

If you know the values of your organisation, take time to consider the following coaching questions:

1. What are your stated values?
2. Where are they published?
3. How are they shared?
4. Are they current, representing what matters to your organisation today?
5. How are your organisational values lived in your everyday activities? Consider how you bring your values to life through stories and discussion with your team.

Activity

Values-elicitation exercise

If your values are a set of words that have lost meaning over time, now is your opportunity to review them and choose to bring them alive, or start afresh and replace them.

To elicit a set of values that are meaningful for your organisation you need to reflect on how you deliver your purpose. Here is a set of questions to kick-start your thinking.

1. What is important about your organisation and what you do?

2. What is important about the way you deliver your service or product?

3. What is important about how you work with one another within your organisation?

4. What is important about how you build relationships external to your organisation?

These four questions can be used as the basis for a group activity. Here is a suggested process for facilitating such a discussion.

1. **Establish how you want to work together**
   Create a Team Agreement by agreeing the values and behaviours you want to encourage so that everyone contributes to the discussion.

   For example:

   Respect is demonstrated by paying attention to the person who is speaking, letting them finish without interruption and switching off mobile devices before the meeting starts.

   Fairness is demonstrated by sharing the time available. Offer your ideas succinctly and create space for others to share theirs.

   Diversity is demonstrated by being open to new ideas and ways of being.

2. Thinking time

In pairs take turns to think and listen. Have everyone consider their response to each of the four questions above. After asking each question sit back and pay attention to your partner whilst they think through their response out loud. Capture a word or succinct statement in response to each question on a sticky note or flip chart.

Swap turns.

3. Gather themes

Collate sticky notes/flipchart sheets and identify themes.

4. Value statements

Generate a discussion, and bring values to life, by sharing work-based stories around the themes identified. Tease out core value words and statements.

5. Shortlist

Decide which words or statements enable you to align most closely with your purpose.

Introduce a voting method to reach agreement, with each person voting for their top three statements.

6. Decide

Decide on the number of values you want to select and pick the values with most votes.

7. **Live them**

Having identified your values, they now need to be lived. Celebrate your values by publishing them and sharing stories that bring the values to life. Reflect regularly on how they show up during everyday activities.

Appreciate people who demonstrate actions and decisions aligned with your values. Provide feedback to develop those who miss opportunities to align.

Take time to lead by example and ensure your values guide your behaviour, conversations and decision making. Reflect on your own behaviour and actions to ensure you stay aligned with your values.

Over time these values become core to your brand: like a stick of rock, your values are at the centre of everything you do.

Pause for thought...

As a role model for your team, take time to reflect on how you are living your organisational values.

How are they embedded in everything you do?

What do you find easy?

What do you find more challenging?

What, if anything, needs to change?

Activity

Personal values

Are you clear about your personal values? What is it that is most important to you about your work and wider life?

If you've never taken time to think about your own values, I invite you to do so now. To complete the following activity, you might find it helpful to work with a coach or colleague.

Process

Start by asking yourself the question "What is important to you about..."

- Your work
- Your health
- Your family
- Your finances
- Your personal development

Take one aspect of your life at a time and capture 3 to 5 statements on separate sticky notes.

Once you have elicited your responses to each of the questions you will have around 20-25 statements.

Prioritise your statements

Now it's time to rank them. Choose one and then decide if the next statement is more, or less, important to you. Do this with each of the statements until they are exhausted.

Once complete, review your top five sticky notes.

Do these feel congruent with what you know about yourself and how you make decisions?

Would you alter any of them?

Are you aware of conflict in any aspect of your life? If so, it may be because of a values conflict. This is when one of your core values is at odds with what you are choosing to do. Something feels wrong and yet you can't always put your finger on why. It is useful to be aware when you are choosing to compromise on such a value. If you are constantly compromising this can lead to stress and anxiety.

For example, if after a full day of meetings you often feel compelled to work late, even though it's your turn to collect your children from nursery, your value around doing a good job is at odds with your value about caring for your family. This values conflict needs to be addressed. If it is ignored and left unresolved, it will lead to persistent incongruence. The impact is likely to cause anxiety and impact your motivation at work.

So, the first thing you can do is recognise there is a conflict and the cause. Once it is apparent, you can make choices. You have the opportunity to consider options and change what you are doing before it becomes a toxic habit. Exploring your choices might lead to a conversation with your partner to change the evening you pick up your children, or you might decide to say "no" to attending a meeting and prioritise getting work done during your regular work hours. By recognising the conflict, you have choice and can explore a healthy response to your situation.

Envisage your outcomes

"If you can dream it, you can do it."

Walt Disney

Now it's time to get clear about what you want to achieve as a team. Together you need to define what will change as a consequence of your working together. This activity is about being clear about the results of your actions. It is not spelling out what those actions are.

Once your outcomes are defined you have a reference point by which to check that what you are doing is taking you in your intended direction. By staying focused on what you want to achieve, you can experiment with how to progress. Staying focused on your end goal enables you, and your team, to make real-time, conscious choices about any adjustments you need to make along the way.

Outcomes are not the same as plans. Outcomes give you focus on an end state without spelling out how it will be delivered. Outcomes allow for greater creativity and flexibility amongst your team. Your team are empowered to respond to what is happening in the moment and make choices about how best to act. Outcomes enable the team to perform by tapping into their experience and strengths and by creating a shared sense of direction.

When you know what you want to achieve, there is a far greater chance of success. In my experience of coaching, when I ask my client the question "What do you want to achieve?", their reply is often a list of what they don't want. We seem to be predisposed to know what it isn't, and have more difficulty knowing what it is. If you constantly focus on what you don't want, it can become self-fulfilling. You start to notice those things are going on all around you. This can be a real issue within a problem-centric organisation. When you focus on the problem, you notice more of the problem.

Tip this on its head and instead, focus on the solution. Describe the outcomes you want to achieve, harness energy and work towards this desire instead.

So, if you are to inspire your team, it's really important that you define the change you want to achieve and how you will know you have been successful. Even better, engage your team in the process and develop well-formed outcomes, together.

Well-formed outcome

The well-formed outcome process can be used to set outcomes for yourself, as well as giving you a winning formula to engage with your team. This is a really valuable team activity that helps your team think through what is required of them and take ownership for their key deliverables. You can also explore how your outcomes connect back with the purpose of your team and organisation.

Set time aside to facilitate a session based on the coaching questions in this chapter. Bring your outcomes to life and get your team engaged in formulating how together you will successfully achieve what you need to deliver.

Activity

Forming outcomes

Here is a process you can adapt and implement to engage your team. The skills and behaviours for you to facilitate this activity are elaborated in Part 3 of the book.

To facilitate this process, you will need flip chart, paper, pens, sticky notes and room to move around.

1. **Identify what you want to achieve**
   Start by gaining consensus about

   *"What specifically do you
   want to achieve?"*

   Think big!

2. **Test**
   Check the statement you have defined and ask yourselves

   "Is it within your control?"

   If not, reframe the outcome.

3. **Create an outcome statement**
   Make sure the outcome is specific.

   State what you want as if you have achieved it already.

   An example of a well-formed outcome that a leadership team might be working towards is

   *"Our team are delivering a
   customer focused service that
   is delighting our clients."*

   This outcome is within the control of the team. Detail will be added to this statement as you continue through the evidence procedure below. This will enable you to get really clear on your motivation and how you will develop your approach.

Moving through the next steps helps to bring your outcome to life in a way that enables you to visualise being successful. At this stage you may not know how you intend to develop and that is fine. Trust that once the outcome is clearly defined, you will tap into the resourcefulness of your team and "how" will emerge.

4. **Specify evidence procedure and measures of success**
How will you know when you have achieved your outcome?

What will you see, hear and feel?

How will others know you have achieved your outcome?

What will they see, hear and feel?

5. **Check motivation**
What is important to you about your outcome?

What will this outcome give you or allow you to do?

6. **Check it is relevant**
Does this outcome support your overall purpose?

7. **Check resources**
What do you need in order to achieve your outcome?

What/who does your outcome depend on?

8. **Check barriers to success**
   What has stopped you from achieving this outcome so far?

   What will you now have to do differently to achieve it?

9. **Future pace**
   When will you have achieved your outcome?

   Looking back from then, what was the first thing you did?

   When did you do it?

   What else...?

10. **Monitor progress**
    How will you measure progress?

11. **Reality check**
    Is this outcome realistic and achievable?

What can you do?

Once you have an agreed set of outcomes, these can form the basis of values-based conversations with your team. These outcomes are performance enablers, providing the opportunity to bring the team together and provide direction, share successes and ask for support. I'll cover more about how you can do this in the next chapter.

Pause for thought...

How are targets and outcomes usually determined in your organisation?

How much engagement and ownership of your team outcomes do you encourage across your team?

What is the dominant leadership style in your organisation?

How aware are you of your dominant behaviours when you get together with your colleagues and team?

How aware are you of the impact you have?

In Part 3 of this book I share ideas intended to get you thinking more deeply about your leadership style. As you move through this book take time to reflect and become more aware of your dominant style. Reflecting on key events at the end of each day can be helpful. Note your habits, impact on others and responses to different situations.

CHAPTER FIVE:

*"Engaged employees are in the game
for the sake of the game; they believe
in the cause of the organisation."*

Paul Marciano

Without meaningful engagement how can you expect great
performance?

***

*Paul needed someone to listen. He felt despair following yet
another performance review conversation with his manager that
left him feeling he didn't matter.*

*So I listened as Paul relayed how he felt his manager was doggedly
sticking to company process and setting objectives that made no
sense at all. In Paul's long experience in the company, objectives
were additional tasks that added little or no value to the daily
work that he was expected to deliver. Yet, what infuriated Paul
was that his performance would be rated on whether or not he
completed these objectives. He challenged his manager about the*

value of what he was being asked to do, but his manager wasn't listening. Instead, duly following process, he was determined to pass these activities on regardless of the impact on Paul.

The impact, as you can probably imagine, was hugely demotivating. Paul left the meeting highly frustrated, cynical about the whole performance management process and his manager. Disengaged, he was keen to share his poor experience with anyone who would listen!

***

Paul's story is not uncommon. Managers who have become transactional, blindly following process with little thought about human engagement, disengage their team. Without discretion or discussion, targets and performance measures that are imposed appear irrelevant to day-to-day priorities. This lack of engagement with a team member becomes highly damaging. It impacts team morale and is detrimental to overall team performance. At its worst individuals within the team become destructive, contributing to a toxic environment impacting the whole team.

If Paul's manager had paused to notice what was happening with his relationship, the signs were clear he needed to listen more and acknowledge Paul. Maybe alignment could have been reached, once both parties felt they had been heard. Maybe the manager needed to let go of the process and challenge what was being asked of him.

Challenging the status quo requires courage, and right now, if our organisations are to change and value people more, we need courageous leaders, leaders willing to be human, who listen to and trust their intuition. We will explore this theme further in Part 3.

In this chapter there is the opportunity for you to consider how you engage effectively with your team, your peers, clients and suppliers.

1.   Importance of connection
2.   Foster autonomy
3.   Conditions to flourish

The importance of connection

"*I define connection as the energy
that exists between people when
they feel seen, heard, and valued;*

*when they can give and receive
without judgement;*

*and when they derive sustenance and
strength from the relationship.*"

Brené Brown

Jane's story is one of connection and belonging which provide her with the motivation to come to work. It isn't that her work is particularly stretching, or that the work environment, pay or conditions are great... what keeps Jane in her role is her relationship with a senior member of her leadership team.

***

I know I'm genuinely trusted, appreciated and valued by Anya, my manager. Anya is always interested in me as a person. When she asks what I'm up to, she has time for the reply and is genuinely curious. When we get together she shows interest in me as a whole person; we don't just talk about work.

As a manager, Anya is a great listener! She listens to my ideas and gives me latitude to experiment. Our relationship is really motivational and that brings my loyalty.

I often find myself in challenging situations, yet I always bounce back. I know I am trusted to manage these difficult situations when they occur and Anya provides support if I need it. I have the confidence to perform well in an environment that requires me to think on my feet, which can be really stressful at times. I am proud to be a valued member of our team.

***

What I love about Jane's story is that the basis of this relationship is built on being human. Jane's manager, Anya, shows support through her kindness and enquiry. Jane feels stretched by the autonomy extended to her. She enjoys seeing what needs doing and is able to get on with introducing improvements and making changes. Anya appreciates that Jane is competent in her role and can be trusted to get on with what is required. As they have an open and positive relationship both Anya and Jane know that if she needs support Jane will ask. This relationship demonstrates a healthy balance between feeling supported and challenged.

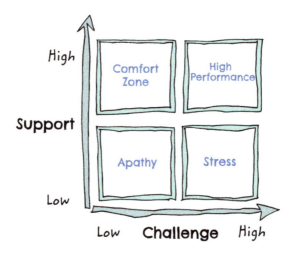

When relationships are suboptimal the results of high support and low challenge are a cosy and potentially unproductive relationship. Alternatively, low support and low challenge may result in apathy or, more commonly, high challenge and low support leads to work-related stress, none of which are desirable outcomes for individuals or organisations. However, if as a leader you are not investing in building healthy connections and relationships, these are the likely results.

Whether your relationships are face to face, or largely virtual in nature, discovering how to connect well, whilst building respect and trust for each other, is vital for great engagement.

Building successful connections starts with intent. When you think about your focus as a leader, are you primarily task or person centred? Traditionally, the focus of many time-poor leaders has been on task and performance, rather than building relationships, which require the investment of time. Building connections has been viewed as a "soft" skill and somehow of less value. This attitude needs to be challenged by leaders in traditional organisations. Behavioural change is essential for these organisations to cultivate a healthy working environment. By building quality connections with your team members you increase their sense of belonging and contribution.

Knowing how to do this and to show up differently can be challenging in organisations where this focus on people, over performance, is not the norm. Developing your attitude, values and behaviours to enhance the support and challenge you provide will be developed further in Part 3.

What can you do?

Here are some ideas to help you to think about how you can connect more deeply with people in your team and colleagues.

Developing your ability to connect will make a positive impact on all those around you.

Inclusion

In Chapter 4 I introduced Maslow's hierarchy of needs model. In the model Maslow identifies that one of our basic needs to function as human beings is to belong. Our need to belong is satisfied when we feel included, trusted, appreciated and valued. When you work in a culture that satisfies these needs, you feel motivated to contribute.

How you treat people on a daily basis results in how valued they feel at work. Your interactions determine whether or not people feel they belong to your team. Making time to get to know your team individually, and what each person needs to be effective, can reap huge rewards. It is often the little actions you take that will make a big difference to how included people feel.

For example, if one of your team is a working mum, who has to drop children off at school, ask her what time meetings need to start and end. Showing you care and want to accommodate her needs is likely to be highly motivational for your team member.

Thinking about your behaviours, how inclusive are you?

Here are some questions to consider.

1. How well do you know each of your team?
2. Do all your team members feel included and an integral part of your team?
3. Do you only spend time with those you get on with?
4. If so, how might this impact those who think differently to you?

Activity

Team map

How effective are your relationships with each of your team?

Take time to consider which relationships work well and which relationships you need to work at. Here is a tool to help you reflect.

Draw a team map

Place your initials in a circle at the centre of the page and start to map your team members around you. Place the people you have a close relationship with nearest to you and those you engage with less frequently further away.

Relationship mapping

Once you have mapped out all your key relationships, notice what the map is telling you.

Scale your relationships

On a scale of 1 – 10, where:

1 is a non-existent relationship, we never engage, and 10 is we engage regularly and there is high support/high challenge for this individual,

- How would you rate each of your key relationships currently?
- Where would you like them to be?
- What, if anything, needs to change?

Review

Review your map regularly to reflect on changes in your team and relationships.

Add new connections and check the health of existing relationships.

How effective are they?

Deepen connections

For you to develop a high performing team, invest in deepening your connections and getting to know your team members better. This means as a leader broadening your focus, so your relationships are on more than the projects and tasks people perform. It means taking time and being interested in the whole person and their wider life. You could start by finding out:

1. What are your team members passionate about?
2. What wider interests do they pursue outside work?

Taking time to find out what makes people tick can help you align them to roles they are best suited to. You will be tapping into their passions and strengths and unlocking more of their potential. It also helps you to appreciate differences. Not everyone is motivated or engaged in the same way you are. Getting to know your team members as individuals means you can flex your leadership style. When you support and challenge people to meet their individual needs, you will be supporting each and every team member to flourish.

Many teams are not co-located which can create additional challenges for leaders. If this is true for you, consider how best to connect with remote team members. Discover how to make use of technology to ensure people feel included in team discussions and events, even if they can't physically be present.

Pause for thought...

When you think about deepening your connections with your team, colleagues, peers and wider stakeholders, what are your initial thoughts?

How effective are your current interactions and relationships with each of your team and peers?

What already works for you?

What actions and behaviours deliver best results?

What do you perceive any barriers to be?

How will you overcome them?

Reflecting on each of your key relationships, which ones need to change in some way?

What would you like to have happen?

How will you influence the relationship?

Stories into action

To deepen your connection, encourage storytelling between team members. Sharing stories helps to deepen your sense of connection as you grow to understand one another better. Storytelling is an opportunity to understand what drives your colleagues, notice shared values and provide support. It can be particularly powerful when you relate your stories to the values and purpose of your team or organisation.

As a team, consider coming together regularly to share stories of challenge and success. This helps to build trust and belonging amongst the team.

Sharing successes gives you the opportunity to celebrate and appreciate one another, recognising the progress of individuals and the team as a whole.

Sharing challenges provides the opportunity to support one another in a non-directive way. The idea here isn't to fix issues for each other; remember most people don't appreciate being told what to do! The idea is to allow the person to share their experience out loud and make sense of what is happening for them. The challenge for the team is to pay attention to the person sharing their story and to listen, without interruption.

Once the individual has shared their story, if they require support from their team members, then there is an opportunity to support the individual using peer learning techniques.

Peer learning process

This is a simple process that generates a real sense of being supported by your peers. It encourages autonomy and the opportunity for independent thinking.

1. The person requiring support succinctly shares their story.
2. They then pose the problem they are grappling with as a question they would like their colleagues to consider.
3. Each of the team takes a turn to share a story from their own experience of a similar situation and how they approached it. The intention is to provide a fresh perspective to the issue, NOT to give advice. If you have nothing relevant to share, simply "pass" on your turn.
4. Once the round is complete the person presenting the original story has a chance to reflect on the stories they have heard and reflect back what they are taking from the learning experience that will help them.

Meet on purpose

*"A manager's ability to turn meetings
into a thinking environment is probably
an organisation's greatest asset."*

Nancy Kline

So much of our time at work can be taken up in unproductive, soul-destroying meetings. There is huge opportunity to change the nature of how we meet. When you meet on purpose, introduce simple practices and are intentional about your behaviour, you can positively impact the health and productivity of your meetings.

Meetings are often thwarted by well-intentioned leaders who think they know best or feel the need to solve today's challenge. These leaders believe the group around the table expect them to lead and be in control. Meeting cultures quickly deteriorate into an example of a high command, high control. In these situations engagement is diminished and value for participants is minimal.

Before embarking on any meeting, think about why it is required. Be clear about your purpose for the meeting. Once clear about the purpose for bringing people together, think about the behaviours you need to model to get the best from everyone. Is this the right time to give direction, or do you want people to engage and contribute? Consider how best to flex your style to meet the situational requirements.

You are far more likely to engage your attendees by giving everyone the opportunity to contribute. Make sure you pay attention and listen to updates with genuine interest and curiosity and without interruption. When the conditions are right, you harness the potential in the room and enable new thinking to emerge.

Far more engaging is the leader who takes a facilitative approach. Rather than prescribing solutions, they encourage everyone to have a voice and to think about their personal contribution to the discussion.

If you regularly host meetings here are some helpful practices for you to experiment with:

1. Before you meet be clear about the outcomes for the meeting.
2. Get your meeting off to a good start.
3. Create a healthy meeting environment.
4. Run your meeting effectively.

What can you do?

Here I share an example of an effective meeting process which encourages the facilitator to adopt behaviours in which everyone feels valued for their contribution and safe to engage.

Know your outcome

If meetings are taking up a significant proportion of your working week, you need to examine why. If not carefully managed, attending meetings can sap energy, leaving people feeling unproductive and demotivated.

Common complaints I hear include:

- Meetings lack focus.
- Two or three voices dominate.
- You leave the meeting feeling unheard, having been unable to contribute your knowledge and experience.
- It was a waste of time.

So perhaps the first thing for you to consider is, is this meeting really necessary? Is there a more effective way to achieve your intended outcome? If the meeting is deemed necessary, get it off to a good start by being absolutely clear about the purpose of your meeting.

Why are you meeting? What do you want to achieve?

For example, do you intend to:

- Share information?
- Make a decision?
- Create ideas?
- Explore feedback?
- Learn from one another?
- Something else?

Once clear about whether a meeting is needed and has a clear purpose, you will be able to keep the meeting focused and on track.

Get your meeting off to a good start

Every meeting you chair is an opportunity to harness the collective energy and wisdom of the individuals in the room.

Who should attend?

So often people sit in meetings out of habit with nothing to contribute. Think carefully about who should attend your meeting. Consider only inviting people who will either contribute to delivering your meeting outcome, or will benefit from being present and hearing any discussions first hand.

Before participants arrive

Encourage participants to think about the meeting before they arrive.

One way to get people thinking about the meeting beforehand is to share why you are calling the meeting and your outcome. Be specific about what you want them to contribute by capturing each agenda item in the form of a question.

Example agenda

The purpose of the meeting is to generate ideas to improve team performance.

Item 1: Welcome and check-in.

Item 2: How do we want to work together in our meeting today?

Item 3: How do you think we can improve engagement and performance in our project team?

Item 4: What now?

Item 5: Check-out and close.

Circulate the agenda and any pre-reading with enough time for people to prepare.

Note taking

Agree the process for making and recording decisions as part of the discussion about how you want to work together. Decide how notes are to be captured and circulated. Assigning a scribe to visibly capture decisions and actions as they are made helps to ensure everyone leaves the room with clear expectations. The value of having one person assigned to note taking means there is only one agreed record of the meeting.

An added benefit is having an assigned scribe eliminates the need for participants to make multiple sets of notes during the meeting. Switching off technology encourages everybody to be more present.

Create a healthy meeting environment

Here are some ideas, key to building engagement, for you to explore:

Be on time

Respect everyone's time. Your meeting is finite so plan and use it wisely. Start your meeting on time and finish when you say you'll finish. People will have other commitments to attend to outside your meeting.

Agree ground rules

Cultivate a healthy environment in which people are able to think for themselves and contribute to the meeting outcomes. Eliminate poor behaviours from your meetings by engaging attendees in agreeing ground rules and being clear about what is expected. Have an explicit conversation at the outset to agree how people are expected to behave. Time invested up front to agree how you want to work together will pay off in the longer term. Get the environment right and people's thinking, productivity and engagement will improve dramatically.

Things to consider agreeing up front include:

- The roles people will take. How do you want to appoint a facilitator and a scribe? To be inclusive these roles can be rotated and free from hierarchy, giving people the opportunity to develop these skills.

- How you want to behave with one another. Agree what are acceptable and non-acceptable behaviours and make them explicit.

Even if yours is a long-standing meeting, adopting this approach gives permission for any existing meeting rituals to be challenged and redefined by the participants.

Be present

If you have agreed to attend a meeting, show up on time and be present. The quality of attention you give to one another throughout the meeting is key to improving the quality of your meetings. How well you listen, connect with the person speaking and show genuine curiosity about what they are going to say next, will take your meetings to a new level. These behaviours all signify respect for one another.

Eliminate distractions

Agreeing that the meeting environment is to be free from distractions introduced by mobile phones, tablets, laptops, or other electronic devices will hugely improve the quality of the meeting.

Share air time

Respect is born from seeing one another as adding equal value as contributors to the meeting. Everyone has earned the right to attend, to share their thinking, ideas and opinions. The fear of being judged by others can be a huge barrier in meetings and stop people contributing their ideas. The most productive meetings quickly build trust through connection, so that everyone present feels they can contribute.

Show respect for one another by sharing time to talk and time to listen. Listen with an open mind, without judgement or ridicule. If you are talking, be succinct, make your point and allow others time to make their contribution.

Environment

Think about where you are holding your meeting and the facilities required for everyone to be at their best. The temperature of the room, planned breaks, refreshments and audio-visual equipment will all have an impact on the success of your meeting.

Do the people attending your meeting feel valued and appreciated for giving their time?

Run your meeting effectively

Working with the example agenda shared above, here are some ideas for making your meetings more engaging.

Example agenda

The purpose of the meeting is to generate ideas to improve team performance.

Item 1: Welcome and check-in.

Welcome everyone to your meeting and start with a check-in round.

Check-in round

A powerful process to introduce to all your meetings is a check-in. Done well, a check-in brings a positive start to the meeting. This process gives everyone a voice as they introduce themselves and then share their answer to a positively framed question. This simple act of connection helps build relationships and trust which support participants in working through more challenging items on the agenda.

Use of rounds is a powerful way to encourage everyone to participate and contribute throughout a meeting. At the start of the meeting it provides the opportunity for everybody to have a voice in the room and connect with one another.

Ideas for a check-in round at the start of the meeting include:

- Introduce yourselves if you've not met before or new people are joining you. Decide what and how much you want people to share; it could simply be a round of names, or to briefly share your role and where you work.

- To get to know one another more personally, share examples of hobbies, interests or favourite holiday destinations.

- Open a project meeting with appreciation: share something that has gone well for each person since you last met.

Rounds

Rounds can be used regularly throughout your meeting to gather thoughts from participants. To facilitate a round give everyone an opportunity to input in turn. Invite someone to lead and set the direction, either clockwise or counterclockwise. If people have nothing to add to a particular round, give them permission to pass.

Whilst the round is taking place, the rules are not to interrupt, offer comment or get into discussion. You simply pay attention and listen to the person who is speaking, then move to the next person.

With clear boundaries set, the person whose turn it is knows that they have an opportunity to share their insights without fear of interruption. The round moves on without discussion of individual input. This often becomes a generative process with people building on each other's thoughts.

Here are examples of where rounds can be used to add value:

- Gauge opinions following discussions,
- Bring focus to check you are on track,
- Check the mood of the room,
- Ask for ideas,
- Record actions people are taking away,
- Check in and set an inclusive tone for your meeting,

- Check out by ending the meeting positively and with appreciation.

Use them creatively to engage people after discussions and capture the latest thoughts.

Item 2: How do we want to work together in our meeting today?

Meeting agreement

Agreeing up front how you want to work together can be invaluable. Here you have the opportunity to include everyone in forming an agreement and make explicit what behaviours are to be encouraged to enhance the quality of your meeting. This is an opportunity for everyone to take responsibility for creating a healthy meeting environment. Encourage everyone to consider and contribute their ideas about what they need from one another for the meeting to be effective. This can be achieved quickly using rounds, or if you have a little more time, by generating themes on a flip chart.

Ask people to capture individually what they need to be effective during the meeting. Capture each idea on a single sticky note. The use of sticky notes is a great way to engage people and enable them to capture their individual thinking and ideas. Using sticky notes and a flip chart as tools in your meetings can bring fresh ideas and energy to a discussion.

If the meeting is small, you can facilitate a conversation by asking for the emerging themes to be shared and captured on a flip chart. In a larger meeting, get people into groups of three or four and ask them to identify the emerging themes on separate flip charts. Conclude by asking each group to share their ideas.

The themes can then be used to remind one another about the expected behaviours and support to be given throughout your meeting.

Car park

Meetings often derail when discussion points get raised that are not intended to be covered on the agenda. Visibly capture any burning issues as they are raised and agree when and where they will be addressed. This enables the person who raised the issue to feel heard and park their concern, knowing it will be picked up elsewhere.

Item 3: How do you think we can improve engagement and performance in our project team?

Thinking time

Taking time to get clear on your thoughts about a discussion topic can be hugely valuable. We aren't always prepared for everything that arises in a meeting and taking time out to formulate independent thoughts can help to prevent groupthink and ensure thinking stays fresh. This activity can be very focused and time bound. People pair up to explore a given topic for inquiry set by the meeting facilitator. The facilitator agrees how long each turn will last. Depending on the topic this is often around 3 to 5 minutes each way. Managing the turns, the facilitator makes sure people stop when the agreed time limit is reached and that the pairs swap turns.

One partner asks the question posed to trigger thinking, for example, "How do you think we can improve engagement and performance in our project team?"

They then pay attention to their partner, whilst they think out loud, for the agreed time limit. This is not intended to be a discussion or time to ask lots of supplementary questions. It is a chance to feel encouraged and supported whilst you formulate personal thoughts on the presenting question, without interruption. At the end of the agreed time you simply swap over and pay attention to your partner.

Having considered thoughts individually, you can bring the group back together. There are a number of ways you can choose to move your meeting forward, for example:

One option is to facilitate a round in which to share fresh thinking. Each person is given the chance to share what is emerging on the topic for them. This may be what they were thinking in their pair, or they may generate new thoughts on hearing ideas offered by others.

Alternatively, people can capture their thoughts on sticky notes. Use the notes as the basis to share thinking and discuss emergent ideas in small groups or as a whole group.

Item 4: What now?

This is your opportunity to agree what actions and decisions are emerging from the meeting. Check in with the scribe to agree who is doing what, by when, before people leave the room. Where possible asking people to volunteer to take responsibility for an action is more likely to result in engagement and accountability. Encourage people to be honest about the value of actions recorded and to challenge the likely reality of them being completed.

Item 5: Check-out and close.

This is your opportunity to close the meeting positively and ensure everyone leaves the room feeling energised. Complete a check-out round. Ask people to share something they appreciate about someone else in the meeting or something positive they have experienced during your time together. This simple act enables the meeting to close on a positive note.

Pause for thought...

How effective are your meetings currently?

What can you introduce to make your meetings more engaging and productive?

Foster autonomy

*"It doesn't make sense to hire smart
people and then tell them what
to do; we hire smart people so
they can tell us what to do."*

Steve Jobs

If you truly want to engage the people around you, respect that they are creative and talented individuals. People come to work with lots of ideas, skill and experience of their own. It is your role as leader to tap into this. You may find their way of thinking or doing something is not the same as yours. This doesn't make their way wrong or give you an invitation to provide your expert advice.

When you give people the autonomy to experiment and implement their ideas, people flourish. Transferring control encourages people to think for themselves, take responsibility and fully utilise their strengths and talents.

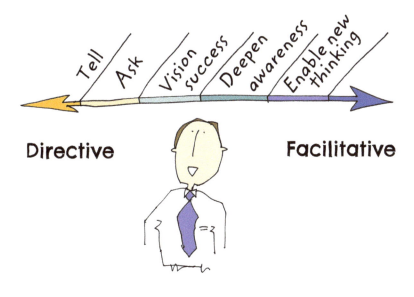

Directive   **Facilitative**

When you think about your own learning preferences, do you enjoy being told what to do and then managed to ensure you do things someone else's way? From an early age, children enjoy experimenting and rarely do as they've been told by a parent. Children much prefer to experiment and work out a solution for themselves. Yes, and to the frustration of many parents, they make mistakes along the way. Many people learn best through experience, by having a go and experimenting. The same applies in the workplace. As a manager you may know what you would do in a particular situation, and often this isn't the only way. Unless you enable your team members to tap into their own experience and creativity, they are unlikely to take responsibility for the outcome. You are more likely to influence your team by asking people if they want your ideas, rather than telling them what to do.

As a leader it is essential you let go of your solution. Whilst it may take longer to begin with, by encouraging autonomy, and supporting your team members to experiment, people will develop solution thinking. In the long term this is a more efficient and sustainable way to address and overcome problems.

There are many benefits likely to result from valuing people for their independent thinking. You will tap into individual creativity to form solutions, which will give energy to the team. Implementation of the solution is far more likely to be owned by the person who is encouraged to develop their ideas. With this ownership there is more likely to be responsibility and accountability to see the job through. I often hear leaders question why their team members are not taking responsibility. This is often a sign that the leader thinks on behalf of their team, without creating space for them to think things through for themselves.

Taking time to think individually, and knowing you are empowered to act on those thoughts to make decisions, has a big impact on trust within the team. The personal learning and growth that comes with this kind of environment is highly rewarding.

For many leaders fostering autonomy is a departure from the way they usually manage. Developing the skills and mindset to be successful is two way. Not only do you need to develop as a leader, you also need to develop your team, so they can respond effectively to your change in expectation of them. Before embarking on this kind of change it is helpful to engage the team in an activity to explore why the change is needed and what it means personally to everybody. Take time to consider the benefits and challenges that fostering autonomy will bring about. Imagine what the new way of working will be like on a day-to-day basis. What behaviours can you expect from each other? Create an open environment where feedback is encouraged so you support one another through the transformation.

To help adapt your own style, one of the most valuable skillsets you can adopt is a facilitative coaching approach. Many leaders think they are coaching, when in fact they are mentoring.

Mentoring is an approach to support your team members by sharing your knowledge, skills and experience, whilst coaching places the emphasis firmly with your team member, encouraging them to think for themselves. When coaching you place the responsibility with your colleague to tap into their experience to find their own solutions to issues and concerns.

As a leader the benefits of adopting a coaching approach more of the time are numerous. Coaching supports a healthy team culture where people are encouraged to think for themselves and take responsibility for their attitude and actions. There are leaders who are natural coaches, whilst most need to be trained. This style of leadership is quite different from the more familiar, directive approaches which dominate most organisations. The mindset and skills required to coach well need to be developed and practised regularly to become a more natural style.

As a leader it is important to find the right balance of support and challenge for individual team members and your team as a whole. It is important to be curious and pay attention to what is happening within your team, without being overcontrolling. Give enough latitude for your team to know they are trusted to work autonomously and learn from any mistakes they make along the way. At the same time, your role as leader is to challenge. Challenge constructively to help stretch and grow the capability of your team. The use of carefully considered coaching questions is a great way to bring safe challenge to your team.

You can start to develop your approach as a coach by engaging in outcome-based conversations. Your focus in these conversations is to be curious and ask questions that keep a view on desired achievements. You are not detailing what you want the person you are engaging to do.

Working in this way gives the people who are delivering specific projects the responsibility to think through what needs to happen and develop their expertise. Encourage team members to connect, share progress and develop thinking with each other. This approach fuels personal motivation to find solutions and overcome any problems the team encounter along the way. Your role is to make sure you remain available to facilitate conversations with your team members that help develop their thinking. Hold back from offering solutions when they encounter problems and trust they are best placed to find the solution, given time to think the issues through. Only share your experience if invited to do so, not by default.

We will explore the core skills required to develop a coaching style more deeply in Part 3.

Pause for thought...

How much autonomy do you currently promote across your team?

As you go about your day become aware of how directive you are in different situations. The spectrum pictured on page 109 can be used to help you make sense of your experiences.

What are the situations where you typically find yourself being directive?

To foster greater autonomy what do you need to stop doing?

Conditions to flourish

How you behave day-to-day at work, and engage with the people around you, determines your success as a leader. There are huge benefits to be gained when people feel they belong and are valued for their contribution. When conditions such as these are cultivated, people are more likely to flourish in a healthy working environment. Not only do individuals enjoy a general sense of wellbeing, people who describe themselves as flourishing are also more likely to be highly committed to their organisation and productive in the work that they do.

So, what can you do as a leader to positively influence your working environment?

Fostering autonomy, as described in the previous section, is a great place to start. The mindset and skills you develop as a coach bring about many of the conditions needed for people to flourish.

Other factors for you to consider include how you:

- Build trust and psychological safety within your team,
- Show appreciation,
- Recognise personal strengths and talents,
- Cultivate learning through self-reflection and feedback.

Let's take a more detailed look at each one of these in turn.

Build trust and psychological safety

"When trust is extended, it breeds responsibility in return.

Emulation and peer pressure regulates the system better than hierarchy ever could."

Frederic Laloux

Building trust between individuals, and within teams, is the foundation for successful performance. Your team need to know they can be themselves and share thoughts, feelings and questions, openly, without fear of being judged or ridiculed. You need to know you can trust your team. You need confidence that they know what they need to achieve and have the skills and capabilities necessary to do a good job.

Creating a healthy environment where people feel safe to admit mistakes and ask for clarity or help leads to high performance. This kind of environment is more likely to result in discretionary effort, where people volunteer to take on additional roles and go the extra mile.

When this happens the foundations are in place for high trust. This level of trust is essential if team members are to be transparent and honest with one another. Only when team members trust one another can conflict be addressed in a timely way.

When trust is present healthy discussions can take place to resolve differences across the team. Without trust, conflict becomes the elephant in the room. Everyone knows there is an issue, but no one is willing to raise it. Left unaddressed, this impacts the energy of the team. Distracted, people talk in huddles and whisper in corners, bringing toxic energy that undermines performance and impacts the wellbeing of the team.

As a concept trust is not easy to define or develop. It is a feeling that occurs as a result of how people experience you and treat one another. For example, if people feel supported to think for themselves, take risks and learn, without fear of retribution, then trust is likely to be high.

As a leader if you show vulnerability and support for the development of others, as opposed to personal gain and self-interest, people are more likely to trust and be open with you.

Trust is formed through developing your relationships with individual team members and your team as a whole. Often, as a leader you can become so focused on tasks and performance that you lose sight of the importance of building relationships. Without making time to get to know one another, sharing experiences and storytelling, your team are unlikely to have a good sense of who you are and what's important to you. Leaders who recognise that being vulnerable and sharing their thoughts, feelings and uncertainty about work-related situations is important, can pave the way for greater connection and trust.

Pause for thought...

How do you experience trust in your team?

What more can you do to develop greater transparency?

Is conflict addressed in your team?

If not, what can you do to create a safe space to explore issues?

Are you confident your team have the clarity and capability to do their work?

Show appreciation

As human beings we feel seen, and our confidence grows, when we are externally recognised and appreciated for our specific efforts. Many people experience being taken for granted at work, which leaves them feeling undervalued. Leaders who focus on performance and delivery tend to overlook individual contribution and effort. Worse still are the leaders who pass off another person's work as their own.

Working in this kind of environment can be hugely demotivating and impacts trust within teams. It is important as a leader to treat people in a way that they know they matter. Making a conscious effort to say "thank you" and reflect on personal successes goes a long way to supporting your team members and making them feel they have been seen and are valued for what they do.

Showing appreciation is a key ingredient to cultivating a healthy workplace culture. Be aware of how often you show appreciation; it probably needs to be more often than you think. If you find yourself offering criticism, or no acknowledgement at all, your team are likely to be feeling quite deflated.

Increase your focus on catching people doing well and let them know you've seen them. Doing this regularly will positively impact on how it feels to work in your team.

Pause for thought

What opportunities do you have to acknowledge your team members for their contribution and achievements to a project or activity this week?

Recognise strengths

As a leader you have the responsibility to get the best from each of your team members. One way of achieving this is by getting to know people personally and discovering their individual strengths, talents and passions. Many leaders underutilise strengths because they haven't made time to really get to know the people within their team. This can be a missed opportunity to help the team and individual excel.

Helpful questions to get to know your team better would be:

- What are their hopes, aspirations and dreams for their career?
- What are they passionate about and where do they get their energy?
- What brings them joy in their work?

It can be difficult to recognise your own strengths as they are so natural to you. Spending time as a team to highlight these blind spots can be really helpful. A simple way to do this is to appreciate qualities about one another. This could be done as a regular round in a meeting or as a conversation to explore team strengths.

This information contributes to developing self-awareness. It can help people make choices which enable them to tap into more of what they enjoy, which is likely to improve performance. When you know each other better as a team, you can work together to craft opportunities for people to flourish in their roles. Developing roles that tap into strengths has a very positive impact both for the individual and the wider organisation. When playing to strengths individuals find greater meaning in their work and are likely to make a greater impact.

Pause for thought

How well do you know the strengths of your team?

How often do you have conversations to explore strengths, talents and role fit?

How flexible are you at accommodating strengths in role design?

Cultivate learning

People tend to flourish when they feel stretched in their role and experience personal growth. Providing opportunities to get involved in new experiences and to master skills is a shared responsibility with your team member. Cultivating a learning environment, without fear of getting it wrong, builds trust and performance.

Learning can be encouraged through regular self-reflection. As a leader making time to support your team members to reflect as individuals and as a team is a powerful way to grow awareness and choice. In many ways self-reflection is more powerful than giving feedback. When your team member owns their insights, they are more likely to learn from their reflections and think about what they need to do to adapt and take action. When someone gives you feedback, you may feel resistance. When you are told you could do something differently, however well the message is delivered, your instinct is to defend what you have done. Being given the chance to reflect on your performance, in a safe environment where you can explore alternatives, has a positive impact. In this supportive environment you are more likely to own your development and learn from your mistakes.

So, to cultivate a learning environment think about how you can stretch people in their roles. Make reflection the norm, where individuals can think out loud about how they are performing. Listen without judgement or interruption as they identify opportunities to learn and improve in the future.

Pause for thought

What opportunities do you have to stretch the skills, knowledge and experience of your team?

How can you support more reflective practice within your team?

How would you describe the environment within your team?

Are your team members flourishing?

What ideas have you taken from this chapter that you could introduce to increase the engagement of your team?

CHAPTER SIX:

Evolve

"*Man evolves himself according
to his thoughts and actions.*"

Swami Sivananda

The leader you are today has come about through your life experience. You are influenced by your upbringing, the society you live in and the culture you work in. Most of this development happens out of your awareness.

How often do you stop to think "What kind of leader do I want to be?" and then go about developing yourself intentionally?

Your experiences form the basis of stories you tell yourself and these stories become your truth, the way you believe you need to be to fit in, perform and get on in your organisation. A lot of the stories told about leadership have become outdated and no longer serve leaders well in modern workplaces. Human beings and the world we live in are developing at a great pace. The expectations and requirements of employees from their employers are changing rapidly and ideas about leadership need to shift to keep up.

In this section I am going to encourage you to be intentional about your development as a leader. Here you will identify the habits and traits you want to develop and do more of whilst making time to consider what you are doing that feels difficult and no longer serves you. With an open mind you are ready to adapt and evolve.

This is important work to enable you to evolve as a leader. I encourage you to undertake this reflection with a coach or form a peer support group. This is an opportunity to bring together a peer group of leaders who share values and are ready to explore their development and support one another.

The chapters in this section will help facilitate your thinking:

1. Who you are at work and your choice to evolve (be you).
2. How your beliefs impact your performance (positive beliefs).
3. How your focus and attitude influence the environment in which you and your team work (choose your focus).

Be you

"Extraordinary things begin to happen when we dare to bring all of who we are to work."

Frederic Laloux

I have learnt that it is essential for my wellbeing to believe in myself and my strengths. Importantly, it is okay for me to behave differently to those around me in the workplace. Developing my self-esteem has been vital for my wellbeing and personal success.

For many years I worked in an environment where I didn't think or act like many of the leaders around me. I believed they were right and I needed to change to be more like others. I thought I needed to be tough, be more focused on performance and do whatever was necessary to deliver results. The expectations I placed on myself caused considerable inner conflict. Ultimately my incongruent behaviour started to impact my stress levels and health. It was a difficult, yet valuable lesson. Eventually it dawned on me: I had to be myself to be at my best. If being my best wasn't a good fit then it was time to walk away from the organisation. I had to trust I would find an environment where I could be true to myself.

Pause for thought

How true are you to yourself at work?

What are you compromising?

So often people experience only a part of themselves at work, as I did, believing you have to behave a certain way to fit in and get on. The danger of this is that you end up wearing a mask whilst at work, your professional persona. You deny being your true self. This leads to holding back, and not sharing with others your true thoughts, opinions and feelings about what is happening in the workplace. If this is the norm in your workplace, then you are working in a toxic environment. Restricting people in this way limits the richness that diversity brings. Instead only narrow views are shared and performance suffers as groupthink dominates. There are plenty of workplaces where people do not show up fully for fear of being judged or not fitting in.

So, what does it mean, to show up fully?

It means being at ease with who you are, whilst being willing to get to know yourself better. When you deepen awareness of your blind spots, you can choose to become more intentional about your style as a leader. With choice you can adapt your style to have your intended impact on others.

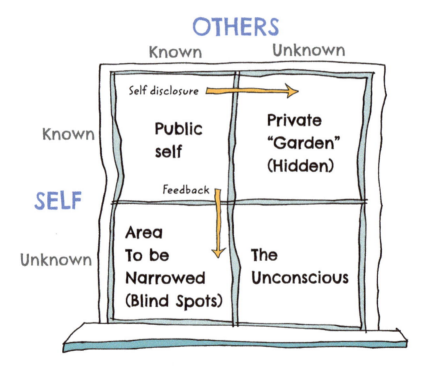

To gain greater self-awareness, give yourself regular opportunities to reflect on your performance.

Pause for Thought

What do you perceive is expected of you?

In what ways do you conform to the group norms in your organisation?

When are you yourself?

It is important to check how you are honouring your purpose, values and beliefs. Are you acting in a way that feels congruent, even if it goes against the organisational norms? If you frequently feel you are going against the grain, it may be time to ask yourself, can you influence change in your organisation? Alternatively, is the organisation right for you? Are your values aligned sufficiently well with your organisation for you to be the best version of you?

When you are working in pursuit of your purpose and values, and you align with what is expected of your work, you can be whole. Alignment leads to self-belief and inner confidence. You know you can utilise your strengths, knowledge and experience to achieve your goals, without fear of reprisal. Your work has meaning and purpose.

Encouraging congruence within yourself and your team promotes:

- High morale
- High motivation
- High quality or service
- High productivity
- Low error rates

- Happiness
- Satisfaction
- Lower stress
- Positive behaviour

Conversely, perpetuating incongruence is a downward spiral leading to:

- Apathy
- Demotivation
- Low interest
- Low productivity
- Anger
- Frustration
- Tension
- Negativity

People are often unaware of their purpose and personal values. Your values drive the choices you make. They are the source of what is important to you. If you have never considered your purpose or undertaken a values-elicitation exercise, take time now to become familiar with what is important to you. Use the "Aligning with personal purpose" and "Values-elicitation exercise" activities in Chapter 4 as your starting point.

Activity

Your purpose

What have you learnt about your purpose, having reflected on the questions in Chapter 4?

Values elicitation

What have you identified as your top five values?

Aligning with these values is key to you performing at your best at work. Reflect on your current experience at work: are all your values being honoured in some way?

If not, what needs to change?

How do your personal values align with those of your organisation? Remember the espoused values of an organisation are not always the lived values. If there is an incongruence, you are likely to feel conflicted in some way. This is a sign that one or more of your values is being challenged. Be aware that over time this can impact on your wellbeing.

Know your strengths

Here are some questions to help you identify your core strengths.

- What are you good at in your role?
- What activities bring you joy?
- What do people ask of you?

- When you perform at your best what does that:
  - Look like?
  - Sound like?
  - Feel like?

From these questions what stands out for you?

What is it that you value about yourself?

Creating an environment where your team are encouraged to bring the whole of themselves to work is important too. These coaching questions can be shared individually, or as a group. When this activity is shared you are helping your team develop trust and respect for one another. You can explore similarities and differences in preferred working styles, and how best to support one another and optimise performance.

Pause for thought...

How much of yourself do you currently bring to your work?

Which of your strengths and talents are being utilised?

If you are denying a part of yourself, what are you denying and what needs to happen to change this?

How can you be more you? What needs to happen to bring more of you to your work?

Positive beliefs

*"Man is made by his belief.
As he believes, so he is."*

Johann Wolfgang von Goethe

Your self-talk can be very helpful and encouraging or conversely quite critical, limiting you and holding you back. As a leader you limit your potential by the beliefs and assumptions you have created. Beliefs are formed through your thoughts and inner dialogue and show up as attitude and behaviour. If you never pause to notice these limiting thought patterns and interrupt them, they will continue to interfere with your performance. Only by becoming more aware will you open up new choices in response, and give yourself the opportunity to practise new behaviours.

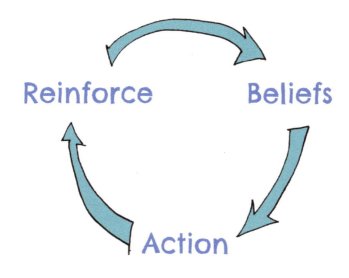

Copyright Julie Hay[4]

Your knowledge, life experiences and the influential people in your life have all contributed to informing your beliefs. Once beliefs are formed you act as if they are true, whether they are fact or not. Over time these beliefs become ingrained and lead to a habitual response. Your response is the actions you take and consequently your results. As the saying goes, if you keep on doing what you've always done, you'll keep on getting the same results.

If you want to improve results within your team, consider what beliefs need to change. This challenge often needs to start with your beliefs as leader. Your team are likely to be reflecting back what they sense from you. To shift beliefs, it can be helpful to focus on what you want (your outcome), rather than get stuck in the problem and what is wrong. We will explore the idea of being solution focused in the next chapter.

As you explored in Chapter 4, defining your desired outcome helps you and your team to define the actions and beliefs required to achieve success. As a leader the beliefs you hold about your team can be key to unlocking your success.

For you and your team to evolve it is important to develop a growth mindset. Your attitude needs to be open to learning and growth. An example of a valuable belief to hold is that each of your team members holds the solution to the problems they encounter. Believing in each of your team and their capability to learn and be creative is central to your success in fostering greater autonomy and engagement.

How effective are you going to be if you hold an underpinning belief that they could never succeed?

Leaders who are aware of this kind of interference and are able to reframe the limiting belief and develop high performance in those around them. Adopting empowering beliefs and attitudes towards your colleagues is fundamental to your success as a leader.

Activity

Reframe a current challenge

Think about a challenging situation at work.

What limiting thought patterns and beliefs do you notice about your inner dialogue?

For example, "Performance review meetings with team members are a waste of time!"

The negative thought patterns and beliefs you tell yourself create interference and limit your potential to overcome the challenge. If you hold on to the belief that you dislike doing something it is likely to be self-fulfilling! In all likelihood you will approach the performance meeting with a negative mindset. You will be looking out for things you dislike; perhaps a "difficult" conversation is required about a performance issue.

To overcome the challenge, what would be useful for you to think instead?

What options do you have to reframe "Performance review meetings with my team members are a waste of time"?

You could instead choose to believe this is valuable time to:

- Get to know my team member better,
- Create space to develop ideas about the challenging project my team member is running,

- Ask what support my team member needs to be successful.

You get the idea!

Now it's your turn.

Start your reflection by becoming aware of a limiting belief that is affecting your performance at the moment. Take time to consider the following:

When you think about a challenging work project or team member, what springs to mind?

Capture your language and self-talk... what do you notice about the beliefs you have formed?

As you become aware of your limiting thoughts, what can you do to reframe your language to form a more resourceful outcome? What would be useful to think instead?

Prepare for your interactions with others involved in the project. Consider how you will engage people by making a list of questions and phrases which convey a positive outcome.

If you catch yourself slipping back into old thought patterns, remind yourself of your positive phrases.

Limiting beliefs can trip you up in all aspects of your life, especially when they go unnoticed and unchallenged. Give yourself time to develop your reflective practice, to notice and challenge these limiting beliefs and assumptions. Experiment with reframing and taking new action.

It can be helpful to identify cheerleaders to support you in any personal changes you are wanting to implement. Find people you trust who will encourage you to stretch yourself and behave in new ways. Who will give you support when you don't quite get it right?

Pause for thought...

Take time to pause and think about your beliefs.

What do you want to believe about yourself as a leader going forward?

What do you need to believe for your team to perform at their best?

What will you choose to believe about your team and their performance today?

Choose your focus

"Problem talk creates problems.
Solution talk creates solutions."

Steve de Shazer

Your attitude to life and work has a significant influence on your impact as a leader. Left unchecked your attitude can do untold damage to you and those around you. If you are constantly negative in your outlook, predisposed to be critical of others and finding problems, you can be a strong influence. The way you show up as leader contributes significantly to the health of your working environment.

Your attitude forms over time; often you are unaware of subtle changes in your mood and tone of language that become habitual. To evolve as a leader, it is crucial that you are aware of your impact on others. By choosing the language you use to communicate with others carefully, you create the conditions necessary to promote a positive environment.

Fault finding has its place. For an engineer, it is an extremely valuable process for solving technical problems. However, when working with people, taking a problem-centric approach often drives negative behaviours within your team. Spending time diagnosing what went wrong often leads to finger pointing and blame, contributing to negativity across the team, and does little to help find a way forward. If you want to improve the way you learn from mistakes and achieve positive outcomes and results, you need to change your focus.

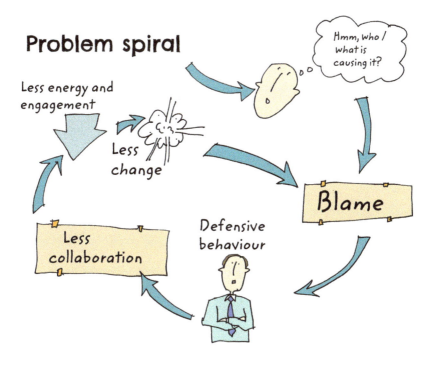

So, what can you do instead?

An alternative approach is to seek solutions. If you recognise that performance isn't where you want it to be, instead of dwelling on the past to find fault, you can focus on what you want instead. This future focus brings more creative energy to the challenge, along with valuable insights and learning.

Solution focus

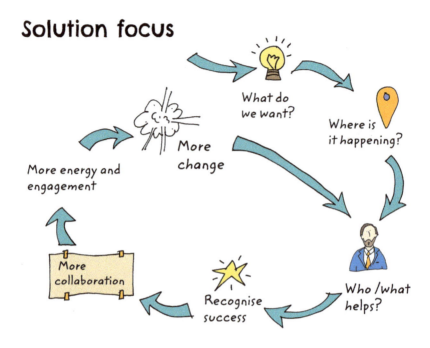

Where are you caught up in a problem spiral? How can you turn it around and focus on finding a solution instead?

Here are some ideas for you to work through in an appreciative way with your team to determine solutions and value everyone's contribution.

Activity

Appreciative Inquiry

Instead of dwelling on the problem or challenge you face as a team, how about experimenting with a more engaging approach to change? Appreciative Inquiry is a strengths-based approach originally developed by David Cooperrider[6]. It can be used to engage team members, and large groups, in thinking about their approach to a wide range of topics.

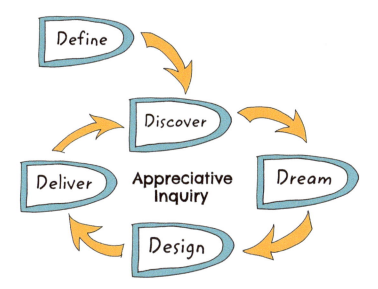

The five steps outlined here will enable you to value your strengths and those of your team. With raised awareness you can make a choice about the actions each of you will be responsible for going forward to move towards your desired outcome.

1. **Define**

   Be clear about the topic you want to explore.

   Your statement for inquiry needs to be clearly defined and stated in the positive.

   For example: "We are a high performing team".

2. **Discover**

   Appreciate your individual strengths and talents, and those of your team as a whole. Share stories of a time when you were really successful, remembering the detail of what worked well.

3. **Dream**

   Now is your chance to be creative and envisage the outcome you want to achieve in relation to your defined topic.

4. **Design**

   This is your opportunity to encourage everyone to think about options and possibilities. Decide what's important and within your grasp. Consider what you can influence and how.

5. **Do**

   Now it's time to agree action and what each of you will do next. Think about what support you might need, how you will share and review progress, how you will make adjustments and celebrate your successes along the way.

Allow yourself time to work collaboratively with this process and for the emergent insights and learning to form new choices for you and your team going forward.

In my approach with clients, I have found real value in working with this process. Here is a case study to bring the process to life.

Case Study

Appreciative Inquiry

In this example of the process in practice, it helped bring a team of ten people together.

Define

The team chose to consider the question:

"How do we maintain a person-centred team approach to our work?"

The question defined the inquiry. The intent of the one-day workshop was to help the team form a shared vision and agree how they could work more effectively to support one another.

The day began with a welcome by the team manager. A check-in round gave everyone a voice, an opportunity to say "hello" and share their hopes for the day. The team went on to agree how they wanted to work together to get the best from each other throughout the day.

Discover

The team moved into the initial phase of inquiry. The focus was on a series of questions to help people define what a person-centred approach involved for them. The team paired up to explore the following questions:

1. What has been your best experience of a person-centred approach at work?
2. What's really important about that experience?
3. What made the experience possible? (e.g. culture, leadership, structure, systems, processes, or something else)
4. If you had one wish for yourself or your team what would it be?

People were encouraged to share detailed personal success stories. Each pair captured their emerging themes on a flip chart. Finally, each team member wrote their wish on a sticky note to share with the wider team.

The team regrouped to present and discuss the emerging themes with each other.

Dream

In small groups the team started by considering "How would our team be if all our wishes came true?"

In pairs they were asked to select a picture card that represented the kind of future they wanted for the team. They then reflected on how the future could be within the team. Sharing their card and personal vision was an opportunity to discuss the attitudes and behaviours required to bring their vision to life.

Each pair captured the core values, beliefs and behaviours they felt were required to bring about change.

Highlights from each pair were shared in a round. The group discussed any perceived barriers and how they would minimise interference.

Design

Pulling all the ideas together, the team went on to design a "framework" that defined the ingredients for a successful person-centred team.

The output from this phase of activity was a flip chart with the agreements for a Team Charter. The Charter was an agreement, by the team, defining how they would work together going forward.

Do

Back in small groups the team were asked to identify specific actions, or changes to processes, that would bring the Charter to life. These were shared with the wider group.

In pairs, each team member declared their personal commitment to live the Charter. Everyone was given time to reflect and identify personal changes in attitude or behaviour they would contribute.

The day ended with a closing round to appreciate one another and the learning from the day.

Process review

Reviewing the process three months later with the team manager highlighted how the Appreciative Inquiry process had been a valuable catalyst for change to the team culture. People were now holding one another to account and referring to the Team Charter. Team performance had improved, absenteeism was reducing and the environment felt far more supportive.

Pause for thought...

How often do you find yourself dwelling on problems, mistakes or challenges within your team?

What opportunities do you have to learn from these situations and re-focus on what you want instead?

Thinking about your natural style, where do you focus more of your energy: problems or solutions?

PART THREE:

Cultivating a Healthy Workplace Culture

"I'm not telling you it's going
to be easy – I'm telling you
it's going to be worth it."

Art Williams

CHAPTER SEVEN:

Courageous Leaders

*"Leadership is not about titles,
positions or flowcharts. It is about
one life influencing another."*

John Maxwell

*B*eing a courageous leader involves letting go of the known and familiar. Often this means unlearning habits and behaviours that are being modelled by the leaders around you. These habits have become custom and practice, the way to lead in your organisation. It doesn't make them right.

Being courageous requires you to question and challenge the way things get done in your organisation. Sometimes this means making choices that will go against the grain. Being courageous requires you to listen to your inner voice telling you there is another way - a better, more human way, to connect with and develop the people around you.

Many of the ideas presented in this book are intended to help you tap into your inner courage, to help you create the space required for you to listen inwardly and reflect more. With this space comes fresh insight, and choice, about the kind of leader you want to be.

The way many organisations have evolved means unhealthy practices, and a proliferation of bad habits which run deep. Fundamental beliefs about hierarchy, power and bureaucracy need to be challenged, in order for more human leadership to become widespread. Many leaders have been promoted into positions of greater influence because they present themselves well. Their position is based on a personal determination to succeed and a focus on themselves. What evolved organisations are discovering is that to be sustainable, in today's modern world, the focus is on "we", the collective. It is time to let go of personal interest and ego. The trappings of status are becoming outdated with a shift to appreciating the value in everyone, based on individual strengths and personality. Modern leaders value people.

In these three chapters I introduce the need for leaders to show humility, let go of controlling behaviours to embrace creativity and experimentation, and choose how they influence their team climate so their team members can thrive.

Humility

> *Humility is "... not thinking less of yourself; it is thinking of yourself less."*
>
> R. Warren

For those leaders who are aware, you will recognise the growing movement towards more human-centred leadership. For this shift to take root, know that in today's world we need leaders who demonstrate humility. So, what does a humble leader do?

Humble leaders break away from the need to be at the centre of the action. Whilst you may have expertise, you do not need to be all-knowing and first to offer answers. Instead you are willing to be vulnerable and curious. You embrace the people around you, encouraging them to contribute their ideas and knowledge. You care about the contribution of the people you work alongside. You are willing to invest in others, putting their needs before your own self-interest. You are wholly aligned with the purpose of your organisation and are willing to challenge constructively when others appear out of step.

When working with humility, you appreciate that unless you are inclusive and invest in the strengths and talent of all of the people around you, individuals suffer. Your ability to engage people ultimately impacts on the performance and sustainability of your organisation.

To be a humble leader you need to let go of the need to be heard, to be right, to do things your way. Instead you build trust and respect by listening in a way that encourages those around you to generate new thinking, inspires the ideas of others and gives people the freedom to act. You listen in order to encourage ownership and respond to what's needed of you. In this way, you provide a healthy balance between support and challenge, to aid the growth of your team. This kind of behaviour creates the foundations for a coaching approach.

You recognise that to be more effective you support others to think for themselves, much more than you tell them what needs to be done. When you let go of your need to share your answer, you develop your ability to trust your team. By adopting an approach that encourages your team to think for themselves, more of the time, people respond positively and creatively. They trust each other more, respect you more, feel more valued; they perform, take responsibility and grow as individuals.

What does this mean for you?

For many it is learning to tame your ego. Left unchecked your ego can create significant interference when you attempt to work collaboratively with others. It forms your inner voice that wants to be heard, be first, be seen. Your ego drives you to be competitive and pushes you forward to get your needs met, before considering the needs of others.

As a leader be aware that your ego is an integral part of you. Through the process of reflective practice, you can listen to your ego, and choose to act, or to let go. A great question to help you do this is "Whose agenda am I on?" This question helps you to determine if you are acting on your needs or in service of the person you are supporting.

If your response is that you are satisfying your needs and curiosity, then your focus is quite clearly on your agenda. What can you do to put your colleague first? You could try being curious about their emerging thoughts and ideas. By creating a generative atmosphere, where you listen with respect and build on each other's ideas, you can release your grip on being "right" and your outcome being the only way.

Pause for thought...

Reflect on an exchange you had during your day. Whose agenda were you on?

Were you attached to your stance, considering only what you wanted to gain from the exchange, and waiting to respond?

Or did you listen to your colleague with curiosity, willing to fully appreciate their point of view, value a different perspective and show flexibility in your response?

Constructive experimentation

"Change is disturbing when it is done to us, exhilarating when it is done by us."

Rosabeth Moss Kanter

To develop as a courageous leader one of the hardest things many people face is challenging the way things are done in their organisation. When you are part of a wider organisation and system, the idea of changing the way things get done can feel insurmountable, so you end up paralysed and do nothing.

What is key to implementing any change is to decide what you can and want to influence and then construct an experiment. This was the approach taken by one of my course participants. Here is her story.

***

... and there it was, my light bulb moment!

I checked out of the Team Coaching training module and it suddenly dawned on me. Adopting a coaching approach has the potential to transform my audit feedback meetings.

The problem

The problem with being an auditor is nobody likes it when we report back our findings. Being told you are not doing well, or you are getting something wrong, makes most people defensive. Even worse, is then being told by an "outsider" how to put things right.

Permission to experiment

My light bulb moment was on realising coaching turns my role on its head. Instead of compliance I can encourage engagement.

Through a creative process, the people best placed to implement the changes can think for themselves. By adopting a coaching approach, I demonstrate belief that the team being audited have the answers to my findings. Given the right environment they are able to recognise what is required and take ownership for their own recommendations.

I had the opportunity to test out my ideas, and experiment with a new approach, with a recent fire safety audit. The outcome was profound.

My intent, to facilitate a very different style of audit feedback meeting. I felt vulnerable taking a new approach. I was very unsure how it would be received. I also felt brave, convinced that the potential to transform the response from my colleagues to audits was worth the risk.

My invite to participants was the first outward sign of the experiment and change to my approach. I clearly stated the purpose for the meeting in advance. I posed questions to get them thinking about the audit findings, even before they arrived in the room.

We started the meeting appreciatively, by checking in with the question "What are we doing well?"

When eventually challenged, "so what are your audit recommendations then?", I gave my reply, "I'm not making any!", surprising everybody.

Instead, I went on to encourage open and honest conversations. Together, we considered the question "What needs to be done differently?"

Everyone was encouraged to have a voice and the discussion flourished. Behaviours shifted from the traditional defensive stance, to one of respect and appreciative inquiry, exploring new thoughts and possibilities.

Results

The meeting was a huge success. Behaviours transformed. Being asked "What are your thoughts?" really encouraged participation and engagement in finding solutions. So much so the group agreed they want to establish a short-term steering group to define their recommendations to address the audit findings.

This is a brilliant example of a self-managed team, clear about their purpose and established to deliver a very specific outcome. No one asked the group to do this; they demonstrated self-leadership as a result of the team coaching approach.

What is the likelihood of the safety recommendations defined by the Steering Group being implemented in a timely way? Probably far greater than if they had been told to comply with third party recommendations being imposed on them!

The future

With this new awareness I can honestly say that a coaching approach has led to results beyond my expectations. I have experienced first hand how my training to develop a coaching approach has impacted on my behaviours. It is making a difference to how effective I am in my role. I am really encouraged by this experience and will be adopting this change of approach more widely for future audits, and within my own team meetings.

***

This is an inspiring story that I hope will encourage you in your own experiments. It is a great example of how you can initiate change.

Stories, such as this one, help build support for your ideas. Who else gets what you get and recognises the need for change? Support one another to create noise around the topic. Get people talking and sharing real stories to constructively disrupt the status quo. These stories could be as a result of having read an article about something you would like to try, or having visited another organisation and observed the way they do things differently. When introducing experiments, keep your energy focused on the positive. What I mean by this is focus on what you want to change to, without dwelling on the negative ways things are currently done. Start small and chalk up some successes. You could begin by taking one of the activities from this book and finding people who are willing to support you to try them out.

Pause for thought...

It is the success stories and connection with your team and colleagues that will enable you to bring about change to your working environment. To create your own experiments, first think about what you want to change and why.

Be clear about the need for change...

What do you want to work on first?

What is your purpose and vision for change?

What is your story for change and who will you share it with?

... and your approach:

How will you launch your experiment?

How will you encourage participation and engage people?

Are new skills and capabilities needed? Do you need to educate people in some way and get their ideas?

What are the tools and techniques you want to employ to help bring about the change?

What have you learnt from the chapters in this book that will support you?

Pause

In a world that seems to demand your immediate attention for everything, many people are connected almost 24 hours a day, 7 days a week. If you don't disconnect to pause and reflect, the quality of your thinking diminishes. You find yourself reacting to notifications, and this unhealthy connectivity to others runs your life.

Most leaders feel time-poor and under pressure to get things done. This constant demand on your time impacts how present you are when with people. Your electronic devices and workload are a constant source of distraction. Left unaddressed these distractions negatively impact the quality of interactions within your team.

Harnessing the power of the collective can seem like an impossible task for many leaders. Individuals work alongside one another within a team by name only. They haven't found the magic formula to perform well together. So, what can you do as a leader to galvanise the performance of your team?

One of the most profound things you can start doing is to improve the quality of your attention towards others. Make time for people, turn off your tech and give the person, or people, you are with your full attention. Agree the time boundaries and know you won't be disturbed.

So, what if you slow down and pause more often? Will it adversely impact your performance, or will you surprise yourself and find you actually speed up?

One of the lessons that really impacts participants on my development programmes is how I model ease. What I mean by this is I consciously deliver minimal content and ensure that people have quality time to engage in discussions with one another. I request that people turn off their tech whilst we are together and make no apology for the pace of my delivery. To start with, this slowing down is quite uncomfortable for some people. For my part it is intentional. What I have found is it helps to build a trusting learning environment where participants feel safe and are open with one another. By slowing down to think about the concepts being introduced, they learn as much from one another as they do from the content of the programme.

For those people who take this lesson out into their working environment, they experience that it has really positive effect. What they report is they are able to quickly build deeper trust within their team and slowing down improves their ability to make good quality decisions. With practice they embed the changes to their routine, creating regular time to pause, think and reflect with one another.

Taking time to pause and really get to know one another is key to you building a high performing team. Start by sharing personal stories about what is important to you about your work. This sharing helps to generate a shared sense of purpose. You are seeking to build connectedness and in so doing, develop team members who value and respect one another for their differences as well as their complementary skills.

Placing importance on learning about one another, about your passions, values and expertise, deepens people's sense of belonging. You build a team who value one another. With deeper relationships, people feel mutually accountable for delivering performance outcomes, especially when these have been agreed up front by the team.

Leaders who recognise their role is to facilitate this high degree of ownership and autonomy are more likely to be successful in achieving high performance. Investing time in forming your team is a far healthier and more productive alternative to allowing them to perform as a disparate group of individuals.

Think about how you can engage with your team in this way. How will you bring your team together to start a conversation that will deepen connection?

Pause for thought...

Here are some questions to help you reflect on your relationship with your team.

Mindful practices

What does it feel like to work in your team? Think about your response from your perspective and also from the perspective of your team members.

How well do you know your team members?

How inclusive are you?

How often do you exceed your performance targets as a team?

Why do people leave?

Do people recommend working in your team?

How would you like it to be in the future?

What will you see, hear and feel when your team is flourishing?

What action do you need to take to be a catalyst for your dream team becoming reality?

CHAPTER EIGHT:

Letting Go

"The leader-leader model not only achieves great improvements in effectiveness and morale but also makes the organization stronger."

L. David Marquet

One of the challenges for many leaders is their need to be in control of how their team approach situations and projects. The opportunity instead is for leaders to recognise the leadership potential in everyone around them. These leaders-in-waiting are often stifled by their environment as they are not nurtured in ways that enable them to thrive. Many people are seeking greater autonomy and personal growth. These people need the support of a forward-thinking leader who sees their potential and invests in their development.

In this chapter I will raise awareness of how you can release control more of the time.

I often encounter cynicism when I suggest that adopting a coaching approach is transformational, both for you as a leader and your wider team. Adopting a coaching approach enables you to optimise the performance of your team. This happens as you foster a learning environment where you facilitate greater autonomy. As you let go of your desire to be in control, you replace control with more engaging traits including listening and experimentation. This is your opportunity to enable your team to take individual and collective responsibility for the choices and decisions they make. This belief is borne out of experience and stories such as Matt's.

***

Embarking on my development as a coach has been transformational. As a senior manager and leader managing multiple services within an NHS Trust, my work is really demanding. I was keen to find a new approach to my leadership style as pressure was mounting. Investing in my development was the best decision I have taken in a long while. It required significant time commitment which I could ill afford with operational pressures. However, I quickly realised the value taking time out would bring. Early in the programme it dawned on me it was essential that I develop my listening skills.

Having time to reflect, I appreciated the need to shift conversations with my team. I wanted to enable them to be creative and think things through together. I learnt that by slowing everything down and giving the team time to think, there is potential to achieve far better results. I changed my language, using open questions and encouraging individuals to think for themselves. They became less reliant on me for their answers and the transformation began. Delighted with our progress, it didn't take long before the team were regularly coming up with ideas they could implement for themselves, knowing they have my support to experiment.

We have constructive discussions where the team openly share concerns, and listen to one another, without judgement. We have come to know one another well enough now to trust that together we will find a solution and as a team will be successful in our delivery.

Fostering togetherness, as an alternative to the more directive approach I had previously adopted as my leadership style, has resulted in greater trust and openness across my team. Noticeably absenteeism has dropped significantly over a twelve month period, the team have greater autonomy and are flourishing.

Whilst it hasn't been easy to let go of old habits, it has been incredible to witness my transformation, and that of my team, in a relatively short space of time. I am really proud of what we are achieving together. It is a fresh approach for the Trust, certainly not yet the norm, however I do believe we are modelling a better way to lead.

***

What is inspiring about this story is the leader's personal recognition of the need to change. Embracing his development, Matt actively sought opportunities to practise the new behaviours he was keen to adopt. Now an ambassador for a coaching approach within his organisation, Matt talks from experience. He has seen first hand the positive impact it is making to performance locally. This is one of a number of similar stories that give me hope that change can start locally, and you and your team can model the way in your organisation.

Without trust in a team for them to think openly together, share ideas and co-create to bring about improvement and change, teams are not reaching their full potential. When a more directive style is the norm, team members may not align with what is being asked of them. If they are not engaged in developing plans and their contribution is ignored, resistance and a lack of buy-in to what has been directed is likely. The impact is low morale as individuals feel unimportant, their contribution irrelevant. If a directive style of leadership is the norm, growth is stifled and people are unable to think for themselves. There is a lack of creativity and people become passive whilst waiting for instructions. The culture becomes constrained and ultimately toxic. Human beings need stimulation, to be given the conditions in which to think for themselves and be creative, in order to flourish.

Recognising the limitations of a directive style, giving expert advice and developing followers, more enlightened leaders appreciate the need to change this behaviour. They welcome learning how to shift to a less directive, coaching approach and developing teams who behave like leaders. As this shift starts to embed, I receive plenty of feedback about the tremendous benefits being experienced by both the leader and the people they are developing as leaders.

Fundamentally, coaching is about truly believing that the person you are working with has the answer. By taking time to support the person develop the quality of their thinking, they will determine their own solution, decide what they need to do and identify what support, if any, they need. By making conscious choices they are more likely to reach a decision, act and be accountable for the changes that need to be implemented. Work becomes a far more fulfilling place when you are encouraged to operate in this way.

People who coach find it helps them build and deepen relationships. Listening, and being genuinely curious, enables you to appreciate the person you are working with. This is a really human act that says implicitly "I see you and you matter". In our time-poor world, one of the failings in our organisations is insufficient time for individuals to feel noticed. One of the excuses I hear time and again for not coaching is that it is far quicker for the leader to tell people what to do. In the short term this may be true, however the consequences are that you are not training your team to think for themselves and take responsibility. Your need to get things done quickly, rather than effectively, means you limit the potential of your team. You become a bottleneck with so many activities and decisions needing escalation for your input and advice, increasing your workload, and so a downward spiral is formed.

There are many benefits in taking time for people, not least of which you get to discover their interests, talents and potential. This can be highly valuable when looking to build on strengths within teams. Tapping into potential is a win for you as leader and builds confidence and fulfilment in your team member.

Overall, the act of coaching is highly motivational and inspires the people you coach to perform highly.

So, what stops leaders from coaching more of the time?

Leaders may have an idea they know how to coach and think they do coach. However, people often come to development programmes to explore the skills of a coach and realise that what they thought was coaching is in fact mentoring. They underestimate how much practice is needed to move away from old habits, where they provide solutions, to leading with a different style. The basic skills of a coach appear to be common sense, however they are not common practice. When under pressure it can be a real challenge to listen well and not provide your solutions. Think about your own style. Are you constantly driven to "hurry up" to create immediate outcomes and solutions, with no time to think?

It's only by slowing down to make time for the people you lead that you will truly enable them to grow and perform to the best of their ability.

One leader shared with me that he found "developing the ability to remain focused on someone else takes real practice". He likened it to "training a muscle at the gym - your purpose is to break the muscle down, so it repairs and grows back stronger - expect there to be pain whilst going through the process. It's the reason we put our seat belt on before we take off in a plane - expect turbulence, but once you're above the clouds it's often plain sailing!"

Leader as coach

*"Coaching is unlocking a person's
potential to maximise their own
performance. It's helping them to
learn rather than teaching them."*

Tim Gallwey

Throughout this book I have invited you to reflect on your leadership style. Many of the suggested practices are intended to help you develop a more supportive leadership style, enabling you to move your team towards being more autonomous.

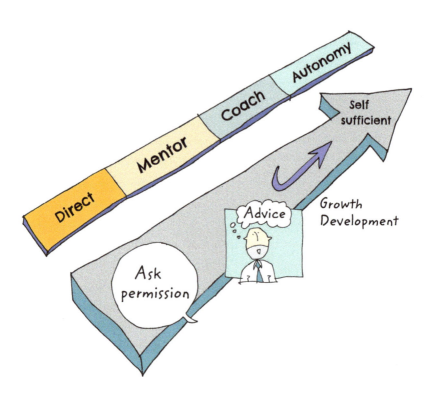

Consider your current style. Where do you spend most of your time?

What might it be like if you move along the arrow?

What would change?

Direct

Many leaders assume that, due to their experience and positional power, they need to take the position of expert. Traits include spending time telling colleagues what needs to be done and how. In meetings these leaders take up a lot of time sharing their opinions and taking a directive stance.

Take a moment and think about the last time someone told you what to do and how to do it. How did you respond?

Most people react quite negatively when regularly told what to do.

There are situations when a leader needs to take control and be directive, to share their knowledge and experience. However, this approach needs to be used sparingly if you are to encourage your team to grow. It is an overused behaviour from habits formed observing traditional leadership traits. Many leaders deny they are directive until they become more aware of what it is like to be non-directive.

Mentor

When a leader mentors someone, they are sharing their experience and knowledge at the request of the person being mentored. A mentor relationship is an opportunity to work through a situation and tap into the experience of the leader. The person being mentored can assess the value of the experience and choose what they want to apply.

Mentoring can be useful if someone is new to the role and doesn't have the required knowledge and experience yet. If overused, the leader develops a team of people who become dependent on them, constantly seeking support and input from the leader. Instead, once your team member has assimilated the essential knowledge for their role, consider how to develop them to use their initiative and give them permission to act.

Coach

Coaching is a great way to develop people and build confidence. It provides a real opportunity for hierarchy to diminish and for two people to meet as equals. Implicitly, coaching says to the other person your thoughts are important and you matter. It is a humanising and supportive approach.

This story, shared by Rachel, demonstrates this wonderfully.

***

As a director within a large organisation, I am leading courageously and taking bold steps to transform our culture, starting locally. We are investing in developing a coaching approach to our leadership style across the organisation, with varying degrees of success.

Personally, I have benefited from being coached as part of the development programme with surprising results. Coaching has given me time to develop my ideas for my business and think through how to implement change, with immensely positive results. I have also seen benefits arising from my practice coaching people from different divisions of my business. My latest coachee is working with me to explore how he develops his confidence in meetings. He has a real fear of speaking up in front of senior people, his fear based on "getting it wrong and being ridiculed".

Working with my coachee, I have helped him to unpack his limiting beliefs about hierarchy and challenged his assumptions. As we came to close our first session I enquired if my coachee had any idea what my role is in the organisation. He shared that he didn't; it hadn't occurred to him to ask. You might imagine his surprise when I shared, "I'm an Ops Director from a different division!" This was a truly transformational moment for him. His confidence soared on knowing he had just spoken very confidently with me for the past hour! As a result of our first session he has shifted his beliefs about what he can say to people, no matter where they are positionally within the organisation.

Coaching is not a cosy chat, it is about sensing what is needed to build a high performing relationship. It is a blend of support and constructive challenge. What I notice is that when I use coaching as my predominant leadership style, whoever I am working with, is that we both grow from the shared experience.

***

A coaching approach is recognised as quite a challenging leadership style to adopt. It requires investing time in your team members and runs the risk of them doing things differently to you. This approach doesn't always result in getting things right first time. Taking a coaching approach means not relying on your own ideas and experience to move forward. It means investing in your colleagues, trusting they have ideas and answers too. When they are encouraged to think through what needs to be done for themselves, they are more likely to take ownership and be motivated to act. Especially having had a chance to sound you out first will provide them with the confidence to give something new a go. Making time to coach helps create a learning environment too, with time to learn from experiences and think about what would be done differently next time.

Autonomy

Leaders who recognise people for their skills and talents and value their competence help their team to thrive. When teams know they have the autonomy to get things done, they feel trusted and take responsibility for their performance. Teams working in this way are highly successful providing they continue to invest in their relationships and agree how best to work with one another. Forming an explicit agreement about the way you work, develop and make decisions is essential for success.

The key for you as a leader is to build relationships with all your team members based on trust. Trust is developed by being flexible. You need to be skilful in knowing when to adopt each of the four leadership positions. Many leaders don't demonstrate this flexibility. They have a preferred style that has developed into habits over time.

To place trust in each of your team, for them to work autonomously, requires you to be vulnerable. You need to develop being at ease with "not knowing" and become more outcome focused. Rather than managing each step and problem along the way, hold developmental conversations about what is being achieved and encourage learning from reflection. It takes daily practice to get comfortable with this shift in focus when it's been natural for you to be more directive and take charge of situations.

Beliefs of a coach

As a leader adopting a coaching approach, holding a set of beliefs that underpin your new behaviours is helpful.

Beliefs are ideas formed through your internal dialogue, based on your life experiences and the influences of significant people around you. Beliefs can be hugely beneficial when they support your development and extremely limiting when they negatively impact your performance. Once formed, they become habit unless challenged. Your beliefs inform your actions and outcomes. If you hold on to traditional beliefs about what leaders do in organisations you will struggle to change your attitudes and behaviours.

One of my course participants transformed his approach once he recognised his limiting beliefs were stopping him from coaching. Once he started to believe in himself, and his ability to coach, his actual experience of coaching became highly rewarding. His light bulb moment came on realising that the person he was coaching was highly capable and, when he listened, had their own solutions to issues.

What are some key beliefs you need to adopt to be an effective coach?

Here are five beliefs for you to consider to help you develop your coaching approach. With each belief try exploring what attitudes or behaviours you need to challenge when you think about adopting the belief:

1. **The person you are coaching has the answer**
   This is an empowering belief enabling the person you are developing to think for themselves. You can let go of your need to provide a solution and be curious about their ideas instead.

2. **There is no failure, only feedback**
   This belief values the learning that arises every time you find a way of not doing something.

3. **People make the best choice that they can at the time**

When you adopt this belief it helps to remove the need for blame. Believing that others make the best decisions and choices possible, based on their present state of knowledge and experience, can be a valuable belief to adopt. If someone makes a poor choice it isn't intentional and is a source of learning and growth.

4. **There is a solution to every problem**

This is a belief to support you to help your coachee develop and grow. Give them time to tap into their creativity to discover their "how". If you create this kind of environment for your team they are far more likely to own their performance and be accountable for results.

5. **The map is not the territory**

This is a metaphor from neuro linguistic programming (NLP) to remind you that your beliefs are not reality. It is useful to remember that people make sense of the world based on their individual life experiences. Perceptions of events and experiences are therefore different for each of us.

What else would be useful for you to believe when you coach?

When coaching your team helping them to positively reframe limiting beliefs can be a valuable way to unlock their potential.

Copyright Julie Hay[5]

When coaching a team member whose performance is stuck, it can be helpful to get them to think about their outcomes. Being curious and asking them to visualise how they will achieve their goal is one way to help them become focused on taking new action and letting go of old beliefs.

Coaching skills

There are a number of core skills that you can develop through regular practice. These skills are vital for forming effective coaching relationships. It is important to recognise the sometimes subtle shifts in behaviour that are required for you to coach well. Whilst starting to develop a coaching approach it is useful to practise the skills and reflect with a partner. A constructive feedback conversation is helpful to explore how you can adjust your style to be more effective.

To engage in a coaching style when working with people, consider the skills you need to practise and develop:

- Build rapport and establish a relationship based on trust.

- Explore new levels of listening without interruption and practise being wholly attentive. Recognise you are listening in service of your colleague and be aware of whose agenda you are satisfying, yours or theirs.

- Hone the quality of attention you give to people to ensure they know they are important.

- Discover questions intended to support the person you are listening to in order to develop their thinking.

- Encourage reflection to deepen awareness and invite learning.

Let's take each of these skills in turn for you to consider your strengths and potential development.

Building rapport

Building rapport is important when initiating any relationship. Being genuinely interested in the person you are meeting and finding out more about them is balanced with sharing insights about yourself. It is important to get this right to ensure the person you are meeting feels positive, having been listened to and appreciated.

Think about a time when you have introduced yourself to someone recently. How did you feel after the meeting?

Was there a good chemistry between you, or did the relationship feel a little one sided?

What was your part in this?

What would you do differently if you were to meet again?

Listening

Are you truly listening?

Having worked with many leaders to support their development as a coach, the one thing I hear most often when they feed back about their development experience is "I thought I knew how to listen until I worked with you!"

We all listen; it's a skill we use every day, and it is useful to be aware that there are different levels of listening.

When coaching you are not listening, waiting to respond. Instead you are fully present, listening with your whole body. This means you are curious about what the person you are listening to is saying, and what they say next. You let go of any judgement or opinion you have about what the person is sharing. You are here in service of your colleague.

This kind of listening requires practice. Even the best listeners are challenged at times to let go of their agenda and inner voice, to be fully present for the person they are listening to. When you develop this kind of listening, growth and confidence emerge in the person you are supporting. They feel valued and heard in the moment. Ideas are generated which leave them feeling engaged and motivated, ready to take responsibility to progress the task in hand.

If people are not used to this kind of listening and curiosity, it may require patience whilst your team and the colleagues you coach develop their ability to think and behave in new ways. If they are used to working in an environment where managers think on their behalf, they will need time and patience whilst adjusting to a new way of working. You might encounter resistance to start with as people turn to you for answers.

You can develop your listening even further by being present for the person you are listening to. Be aware of the wider system and context in which they are operating. By sensing into the underlying meaning of what is being said, you can respond sensitively and demonstrate empathy. Learning to listen fully to both what is being shared explicitly in terms of the words being used, and implicitly in terms of the underlying meaning of those words, is a valuable skill for you to develop and will benefit you in all aspects of your life.

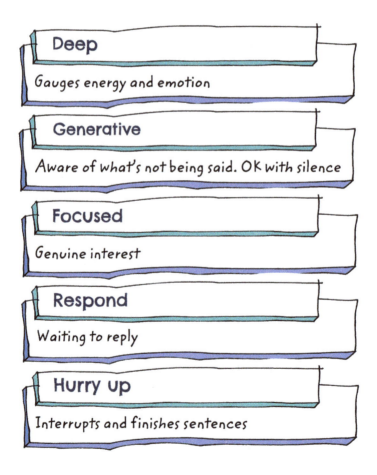

Deep

Gauges energy and emotion

Generative

Aware of what's not being said. OK with silence

Focused

Genuine interest

Respond

Waiting to reply

Hurry up

Interrupts and finishes sentences

Listening deeply, whilst staying focused, requires discipline and practice. Habitually your mind drifts in and out of awareness of what the other person is saying depending on your level of engagement. To stay present and mindful make a choice when you strike up a dialogue with someone to let go of your agenda and be truly curious about what they have to say. As you raise awareness of how well you are listening you will begin to recognise when your mind drifts and make a conscious choice to coax your attention back to the person you are supporting. Stick with it, as like most new skills it requires practice to hone it.

If there is one skill above all others that will make the greatest impact to you in your organisation it is learning to truly listen, without interruption and without holding on to your agenda. When you let go of your need to control a conversation you give rise to emergent ideas and new thinking, experimentation, creativity and trust, all of which are building blocks for the future of successful organisations.

Attention

How you pay attention during conversations can hugely influence levels of engagement by your team members. You have the opportunity to provide the optimum level of support and challenge, which will vary from person to person. This is why getting to know your team individually, and building relationships, is vital to your success as a leader.

The kind of attention you demonstrate creates an environment which says back to the person you are supporting "you matter". The person feels safe and thoughts flow uninhibited. This is sometimes referred to as "holding space".

Attention is very closely aligned with the quality of your listening. Attention comes from listening and then formulating an appropriate response that will enable the person you are supporting to feel encouraged and appreciated. This might be by:

- Reflecting back what you have heard to deepen awareness,
- Asking an insightful question to enable new thinking,
- Constructively challenging something that has been said to provide stretch.

When leaders take time to pay this kind of attention, team members start to feel truly valued.

Questions

When coaching I advise less is more. So often questions are asked based on satisfying your curiosity. Whenever possible keep silent and encourage the person to develop their own thoughts by listening. If a question is needed keep it simple.

Asking a powerful question that encourages the person to keep developing their thinking, such as "What else?", can be really helpful.

When listening to their reply, show you are with the person you are listening to by non-verbal actions such as nodding occasionally or making encouraging noises for them to continue to develop their thoughts.

Before asking a question, check in with yourself; will it be helpful to the other person if you ask it?

There are more tips about framing useful questions in the next section, Unlocking Potential.

Feedback and reflection

Feedback is often perceived as a negative, demotivating experience by people who feel criticised by the person delivering the feedback. Done well, feedback is an opportunity to raise awareness and enable change. So as a leader what can you do to encourage personal growth through constructive feedback?

One way is to take time with the team member being developed. Give them space to reflect on current situations. Encourage them to reflect on their performance and impact on those around them. This way they own any feedback and are more likely to seek support to make changes. Creating a safe environment where reflection is encouraged also builds trust so that feedback is invited.

People are not always equipped to recognise their own blind spots. If being self-reflective isn't addressing the development needs of your team member, it's time to offer feedback. Being constructive when giving feedback means you offer information so that the person receiving the feedback has a choice about what they do on receiving it.

Here is a helpful framework for you to plan your feedback. This four-stage process is useful for giving both appreciative and developmental feedback. Appreciative feedback is showing your gratitude for a specific action or behaviour you have noticed about your colleague. Developmental feedback is intended to help the person identify a potential blind spot and encourage them to think about how they might act differently next time.

Stage 1: Identify a specific behaviour you want to reinforce or change.

Stage 2: Identify a specific situation where you observed this behaviour.

Stage 3: Describe the impact of this behaviour and the consequences.

Stage 4: Give the person receiving the feedback the opportunity to reflect on what they might learn from the situation. What might they change? What will they continue to do, or build upon?

Plan your message and think about your language. Try stepping into the shoes of the person who you want to give feedback to. Imagine how they might feel on hearing your message.

The key to delivering successful feedback is your style and timing of delivery. If you have built trusting relationships with your team, regular two-way feedback becomes the norm. You are modelling a willingness to receive feedback, as well as offer it. Adopting a coaching style when delivering feedback enables you to create a healthy learning environment where people feel supported and encouraged to explore their development and reflect for themselves, so owning any changes identified.

Choosing to adopt a less directive style requires conscious experimentation and practice. Practice is essential for change to happen and for you to embed new behaviours. It is worth remembering that behavioural change usually happens outside your comfort zone. Trying out a different way of being can feel awkward and clunky to begin with.

Pause for thought...

Take a moment to reflect on the leadership positions arrow on page 164. Where do you spend most of your time?

- Direct
- Mentor
- Coach
- Autonomy

What habits have you formed around your preferred style?

What are your current beliefs about being a leader in your organisation?

How might your beliefs assist, or interfere with, your ability to support your team become more autonomous?

What do you want to do more of to enhance your effectiveness as a leader?

Pick a couple of opportunities today and notice your level of listening. What are you aware of?

Unlocking potential

"The simple act of paying positive attention to people has a great deal to do with productivity."

Tom Peters

Adopting a less directive approach can be a powerful behaviour choice available to you as a leader. As you start to adapt your approach become aware of the language you use. Language can have a huge impact on people and their performance. The words you choose, and how you ask questions, can give away a lot about your thoughts on the topic being explored. Your words and tone of voice can be loaded with judgement and opinion.

Learn to frame your language to be appreciative, supportive and encouraging, rather than judgemental, negative and challenging.

When coaching, the type of questions you ask can make a big impact on the resourcefulness of the person you are coaching.

Open questions

Open questions are really helpful. These questions help expand the thinking of the person you are supporting. These questions start:

What?
How?
Who?
When?
Where?
... and occasionally Why?

I recommend using "Why" sparingly as it can feel like a loaded question, one that makes people feel the need to defend themselves.

How might you respond to someone asking, "Why did you do that?"

The person asking the question may be genuinely curious, not intending to attract a defensive response, which may close down the enquiry.

Be aware of any language patterns you may have developed that come across as being critical. Your tone of voice and timing contribute to the response from the person on the receiving end of your question and comments.

One of my favourite questions when coaching is simply "What else?"

This question presupposes the person I am working with is creative and has more to give, which often proves to be true when you ask this question!

The most effective coaching arises when questions are kept simple and succinct.

Closed and leading questions

Closed questions can be useful to pinpoint answers quickly, however they need to be formulated carefully as they can disclose what you are thinking and become leading questions.

> Do you...?
> Have you...?
> Will you...?
> Is there...?
> Are you...?

There are often better ways to ask closed questions, by using an open alternative for example:

Do you think you will be finished by then? or When do you think you will finish?

Have you thought about resources? or What resources will you need?

Have you tried to call a meeting? or What have you tried?

Hypothetical questions

These are great questions to generate new thinking and open up possibilities and choices.

"What would happen if...?"

"Imagine it's 12 months from now, what is happening?"

Positive reframe

Often people find themselves in new situations, doubting their abilities and whether they can do something. If your coachee shares information with you expressing their doubt that they can do something, try reframing their statement. Get them to imagine what will happen if they can.

Here is an example:

"I can't deliver the presentation."

"If you were to deliver the presentation, what would you do?"

Rather than dwelling on problems and feeling stuck, help your coachee find language to describe what they want instead.

"I don't want to deliver the presentation."

"So, if you don't want to deliver the presentation, what do you want instead?"

Gaining commitment

A neat way to test commitment when coaching is to ask a scaling question. If the person you are working with has decided what they intend to do, ask them on a scale of 1 to 10 how committed they are to take action. If they reply with a number less than 10, ask them what needs to happen to take them +1. The aim of this question isn't to get them to 10, simply to get them to recognise they can improve.

Time to reflect

One of the key outcomes of coaching is to support your team member in raising their self-awareness. Provide the space for them to slow down and reflect on their own performance. This is a really valuable way to spend time together, whilst at the same time developing your relationship and connection. Taking time to pause and reflect on the challenges and successes of a project and asking your colleague to consider what they might do differently can be invaluable to personal performance and that of the wider team.

Pause for thought...

Coaching is a real opportunity to connect and provide support to your team member. Done well, they are likely to feel supported, valued, listened to, resourceful, productive and focused... it is powerful.

Consider how you can introduce a coaching style to your leadership more consciously. Identify an opportunity to support one of your team members and enter the dialogue with the intent of listening well. Hold back from judgement and providing solutions. Remember, your colleague will have their own ideas and they don't have to do what you would.

Be curious, and if you think it would help your colleague develop their thinking around the project or task, ask open questions. Importantly, give them a chance to reflect and think things through for themselves.

Following the dialogue, reflect on your own performance...

What went well?

How did you feel afterwards?

How did your team member feel?

How much thinking did your team member do for themselves?

What would you do differently if you were to have the dialogue again?

CHAPTER NINE:

Be the Change

*"We can change culture if
we change behaviour."*

Dr. Aubrey Daniels

For systemic, organisational change to take place, it starts with you.

Prioritising your own growth and development will be a catalyst for wider change in your organisation. You become a ripple and through adapting your style, others will start to change around you. When you choose to deepen awareness about your habits and behaviours and choose how you want to impact the people around you, you will start to transform.

This story of a newly promoted operations director, inheriting a large team, shows that transformation really is possible, once you choose to invest the time to work on yourself.

***

On promotion to operations director, there were legacy issues which demanded my immediate attention. This took some months to address, giving me time to get to know my team. With the issues in hand I was ready to consider how to make changes to enhance team performance. Whilst I didn't recognise it at the time, embarking on a leadership development programme came at the perfect moment for me.

The problem

I was being drawn by my team into operational detail. They looked to me for direction and I was quickly drawn into a cycle of command and control. I recognise now that what was happening in transactional analysis terms is that my relationship with my team was one of parent-child. I was becoming the bottleneck for decision making and the team were becoming dependent on me before taking action.

Permission to experiment

I quickly recognised this style of management was unhelpful and unsustainable.

At the start of the programme I was introduced to Tim Gallwey's performance equation

$$Performance = Potential - Interference$$

The penny dropped for me. Through coaching I could start to address the interference holding back the team.

Working with my peers during each course module provided me with the perfect environment to challenge my thinking. Having time to reflect quickly helped me to develop new positive beliefs, possibilities and behaviours.

It hasn't always been easy, yet I am constantly rewarded by being courageous, experimenting and trying new ways of being with my team.

Results

The impact I experienced adopting a coaching approach was almost immediate. The results far more than I bargained for!

The opportunity to be coached during each module, whilst brief, had an incredible impact on the quality of my thinking. Through the regular coaching sessions with my peers I developed a clear vision for my operations strategy, how the lean structure would operate and what needed to be implemented.

Being coached gave me the chance to leave operational issues at the door and think strategically. I was able to consider different perspectives and how best to engage my team in the changes I visualised. I received healthy challenge from my peer coaches, who were brilliant at holding me to account!

As the course progressed, I started to appreciate the impact that the change in my behaviour was having on my team. As interference such as extra emails under the command and control approach were removed and 360° expectations were set, the performance of the team soared.

As I adopted a coaching style more of the time, people responded by stepping up and being more accountable. The team engaged in building the strategy and team structure with me. This more open and engaging way of working has improved communication across the team. Individuals are much clearer about their roles and responsibility. The team no longer look to me constantly for direction and are now far more autonomous in making decisions. Actively volunteering to join working groups, the team are again demonstrating a willingness to engage and greater self-management. I am delighted that relationships have improved both within my team, across the wider business and with key external stakeholders.

Over the past 12 months the team have received external validation for their successful performance and achievements, ending the year on an inspiring high.

... and the future?

With foundations in place, my intention is to continue to develop the team. Encouraging each and every person to fulfil their potential and flourish in this new environment and best practice sharing, all of which will lead to improved operational performance. I'm excited for what's to come and what we, as a team, will achieve together.

***

If the culture feels dysfunctional in your team or organisation, it probably is!

Trust yourself to recognise the signals. Be prepared to be courageous and model the way. Develop your vision, become more self-aware and be the change needed to bring about excellence in your organisation. You can choose to become the ripple, working to inspire, engage and evolve all those around you.

Use ideas from this book to get to know yourself more deeply and take time to reflect on how you impact others. Remember that much of what you do is habitual rather than from awareness. Grow to be more mindful and purposeful. Make a positive choice to keep what works and work to change what doesn't.

Where is your support?

"Whether you think you can, or you think you can't – you're right."

Henry Ford

Interference arises from the internal chatter that goes on in your mind. You have deeply embedded stories you tell yourself that interfere with you being the best version of yourself. These stories have formed based on your life experiences and from the influence significant people in your life have had on you. You play these stories over and over, until these thoughts form your beliefs and you act as if they are true.

Once embedded your thoughts become the basis of your habits and are often blind spots. Unless you take time to notice these patterns you fall short of your full potential. When you recognise this chatter for what it is you can make more conscious choices to reframe and challenge limiting thoughts and beliefs to change your outcomes.

Where is your support coming from to help you evolve and be the courageous leader our world needs right now? It takes regular daily action to change a habit. It can be really helpful to find coaching support to help you develop. Working with an experienced coach will enable you to be more aware of the power and limitations of your inner voice. It will give you choice and flexibility to challenge yourself and be more intentional. You can choose to adopt new, more resourceful habits and behaviours.

Pause for thought...

As a leader one of the most powerful things you can do is develop your own mindfulness. With practice you can be more present in each moment of the day. Rather than rely on outdated practices, learn to sense and respond to what situations require of you. Learn to flex your style.

The coaching questions asked throughout this book are a starting point inviting you to stop and notice what is happening to you and around you. My intention is to help you deepen awareness and learn from your experiences, to enable you to create more mindful choices in your behaviour. With the support of your journal, and by working with your coach, you will become more conscious about what causes interference, limiting your potential as a leader.

By working with the ideas and questions in this book you will develop your reflective practice. This is your opportunity to recognise the type of leader you want to be and become intentional about how you lead.

Choose a leader you admire.

What is it they do specifically that you admire?

How do they make a positive impact on the people around them?

How do they influence and engage?

Once you recognise these desirable traits in others, with practice you can adopt them as your own.

What will you stop doing?

What will you start doing?

What will you continue to do?

CHAPTER TEN:

Rethinking Leadership

"A sign of a good leader is not how many followers you have, but how many leaders you create."

Mahatma Gandhi

So, if traditional models of leadership are failing, what new thinking will you embrace to become a more human leader?

You have a choice.

Many are not ready to face the problems being experienced in our workplaces, and perpetuate old styles of leadership. Without personal challenge they contribute to the toxic nature of many workplaces in our society.

The alternative is to adapt, to take responsibility for your growth, to experiment and evolve your leadership practice to meet the needs of modern workplaces.

We need leaders who know there is value in slowing down, to pause and reflect, leaders who embrace humanity in their workplace, who connect and build relationships with their colleagues and teams. Are you ready to cultivate a healthy workplace culture by becoming a more human leader?

What will you choose?

Endnotes

1. https://www.mentalhealth.org.uk/news/stressed-nation-74-uk-overwhelmed-or-unable-cope-some-point-past-year

   http://www.hse.gov.uk/statistics/causdis/stress.pdf

   https://www.peoplemanagement.co.uk/news/articles/work-related-stress-jumps-quarter-reach-epidemic-levels

2. https://news.gallup.com/opinion/gallup/219947/weak-workplace-cultures-help-explain-productivity-woes.aspx

3. https://www.amnesty.org/download/Documents/ORG6097632019ENGLISH.PDF

4. Permission has been granted by Julie Hay to utilise the BARs to Success diagram which originally appeared in *Transactional Analysis for Trainers* by Julie Hay, Sherwood Publishing, 2009, page 125.

5. Permission has been granted by Julie Hay to utilise the PRO Success diagram which originally appeared in *Transactional*

Analysis for Trainers by Julie Hay, Sherwood Publishing, 2009, page 126.

6. Permission has been granted by Ada Jo Mann to utilise the concept of Appreciative Inquiry within this book.

About Karen

Karen Mason, MBA, is passionate about growing conscious leaders and on a mission to help leaders cultivate healthy workplace cultures. Karen cares deeply about the experience people have at work and has become a positive force for rethinking leadership. In our rapidly changing world, she believes that leaders have the responsibility to challenge themselves, to grow and develop. She encourages leaders to be open to new ways of organising and behaving in ways that enable their teams to flourish, so that people go home at the end of each day feeling valued and fulfilled.

Described as "bringing enthusiasm and energy to her work, whilst making a difference through the power of honest and courageous conversations", Karen facilitates events that enable leaders to evolve, and recognise how they need to be, to inspire and engage the people around them.

With an operational background in aerospace and defence within engineering and procurement, Karen has always been fascinated by people and how they choose to impact their organisation and the wider world. Through her experience as a leader and facilitator, she has discovered valuable patterns about how people think, act and communicate, and how to create environments in which people flourish and operate at their best. Karen enjoys sharing her thinking in order to facilitate leadership and organisational development and inspire positive action.

Karen operates in alignment with her values of courage, attention, collaboration and learning, and she hopes this book inspires you to pause and rethink your leadership.

Work with Karen knowing she will help you to challenge your thinking in a constructive way and support you to develop your leadership approach.

Contact Karen at karen@karenmasonassociates.co.uk or visit her website: www.leadingonpurpose.org.uk.

Acknowledgements

Thank you...

To all those who have influenced my thinking and experience of being a leader. The older I grow the more I value the lessons from my past. I embrace the growth in me that is happening now and is yet to come.

I'm not the finished article. I don't always get my relationships and connection with others right. There is still much for me to learn about being human and about being a more human leader.

Huge thanks to all of you who supported me in writing this book. My book mentor, Karen Williams, Jon Ralphs, for his wonderful illustrations, the people who kindly completed my survey and those of you willing to read and comment on my early drafts. It would have been a much tougher experience without all your guidance, encouragement and feedback.

Thanks to Louise Close, my thinking partner, for constantly taking me out of my comfort zone and challenging my thinking. Madeleine Allen, for continuing to believe in me when I stop believing in myself. Aaron Mason, for being curious and keen to listen as my thoughts about this book unfurled.

Specific thanks go to the hundreds of programme participants I have worked with over the past 12 years. Your stories of transformation continue to inspire me time and again. It is your stories that have provided evidence of what is truly possible, when leaders adopt a less directive, more human approach more of the time. Without you this book would not have been possible.

Recommended Reading

There are many models of excellence in the world who are bringing greater awareness of the need for more human leadership to come to the fore. Here I would like to recognise some of the thought leaders who have influenced my practice as a leader, coach and facilitator, and in my writing of this book.

Dare to Lead: Brave Work. Tough Conversations. Whole Hearts, by Brené Brown

Everybody Matters: The Extraordinary Power of Caring for Your People Like Family, by Bob Chapman and Raj Sisodia

Appreciative Inquiry: A Positive Revolution in Change, by David Cooperrider and Diana Whitney

Time to Think: Listening to Ignite the Human Mind, by Nancy Kline

Reinventing Organizations: A Guide to Creating Organizations Inspired by the Next Stage in Human Consciousness, by Frederic Laloux

Turn the Ship Around: A True Story of Building Leaders by Breaking the Rules, by David Marquet

A Theory of Human Motivation, by Abraham Maslow

Drive, by Daniel H. Pink

Start with Why: How Great Leaders Inspire Everyone to Take Action, by Simon Sinek

Coaching for Performance: The Principles and Practice of Coaching and Leadership, by Sir John Whitmore

What Now?

To change ingrained habits requires awareness and practice. Having read this book, I encourage you to pause and think about one small step you can take. Pick one technique or behaviour change you would like to introduce and give it a go. Be brave and experiment with a different way of holding conversations, giving people your full attention or running your meetings differently. Allow yourself to be vulnerable and let people know you are trying something new. Ask for their support to remind you when you slip back into old ways. Whilst this takes courage, people will respect you for asking for help.

For additional support please visit my website www.leadingonpurpose.org.uk/pause where I will be adding resources in support of the main messages in the book.

If you are ready to pause and rethink your leadership, I have development programmes available that bring the content of this book to life. These programmes can range from a one-day event to start you thinking about yourself as a leader and what kind of impact you want to make, through to a more comprehensive transformation programme for senior leadership teams. The modules take you beyond the theory and give you a hands-on practical experience that you can immediately transfer to your workplace.

Bespoke programmes can be delivered within your organisation to challenge traditional ways of thinking and help you to bring about cultural change.

For more information, visit the website or email karen@karenmasonassociates.co.uk.

Notes